COUNSELING FAMILIES WITH CHRONIC ILLNESS

Edited by Susan H. McDaniel

AMERICAN
COUNSELING
ASSOCIATION

■ ■ ■

THE FAMILY PSYCHOLOGY AND COUNSELING SERIES

Jon Carlson, Editor

Counseling Families with Chronic Illness

10 9 8 7 6 5 4 3 2 1

American Counseling Association
5999 Stevenson Avenue
Alexandria, VA 22304

Acquisitions and Development Editor
Carolyn Baker

Production Manager
Michael Comlish

Copyeditor
Heather Jefferson

Cover design by Martha Woolsey

Library of Congress Cataloging-in-Publication Data

Counseling Families with Chronic Illness / edited by Susan H. McDaniel
    p.   cm. — (The family psychology and counseling series)
    Includes bibliographical references.
    ISBN 1-55620-144-3
    1. Family psychotherapy. 2. Chronically ill—Family relationships. 3. Chronically ill—Counseling of. 4. Chronic diseases—Psychological aspects. I. McDaniel, Susan H.
    II. Series.
RC488.5.c637 1995
616.89' 156—dc20

95-5670
CIP

The Family Psychology and Counseling Series

Counseling Families with Chronic Illness
Susan McDaniel, PhD

Mid-Life Divorce Counseling
Lita Linzer Schwartz, PhD

Transitioning from Individual to Family Counseling
Charles Huber, PhD

Understanding Stepfamilies: Implications for Assessment and Treatment
Debra Huntley, PhD

In Preparation

Counseling Aging Parents and Their Families
Irene Deitch, PhD

Counseling Substance Abusers and Their Families
Judith Lewis, PhD

Advisory Board

■ ■ ■

THE FAMILY PSYCHOLOGY AND COUNSELING SERIES

Table of Contents

From the Series Editor

This is an important book. For too long, counselors have denied the holistic nature of people and their world. We have acted as if we treat only the mind. With upcoming changes in health care, it is likely that counselors' roles will shift from working primarily with clients and families with normal developmental issues, to dealing with more chronic health problems. Psychosocially oriented professionals (e.g., counselors, psychologists, social workers, etc.) must begin to work collaboratively with biologically oriented professionals (e.g., doctors, nurses, physical therapists, etc.).

Susan McDaniel and her colleagues present their ground-breaking paradigms for dealing with today's tough problems. Each chapter takes a specific area of the challenging work of helping families with chronically ill members. Most counselors have occasion to treat such situations; however, up to this point, they have not had the advantage of proper training or information. This collaborative approach calls for an appreciation of the various roles and expertise of the different health-care professionals, and realizes that the patient and the patient's family are our most important allies. Research demonstrates both the clinical and cost-effectiveness of this approach for patients, families, providers, and the greater health-care system.

This book is long overdue. Please take the time to become aware of these ideas, and consider joining the Collaborative Family Health Care Coalition (40 West 12th St., New York, NY 10011, 212/675-2477).

—Jon Carlson, PsyD, EdD
Series Editor

Preface

F amily therapy has become the mainstream in the 1990s. One benefit of this growth is the opportunity to closely examine the theories and assumptions that drove us during the years when family therapy was on the fringe—when it was fighting for problems to be understood in context in relationship to others. In those days, we eschewed the medical model, as well as most every other thing medical. We disagreed with the reductionistic medicalization of human behavior problems, and with most of the treatments that followed from a medical model theory. Unfortunately, most of us threw out the baby with the bath water. We cooperated with our culture's mind–body split, and we agreed to only touch the mind.

In retrospect, this was a mistake. Now, armored with confidence brought by the success of family therapy in the 1970s and 1980s, it is important to return to the medical arena—to help patients, families, and health-care providers offer comprehensive health care in a rapidly changing health-care market. We now have some colleagues of like mind: health-care providers who also apply systems theory and techniques in their medical practices. These are primary-care family nurses and nurse practitioners, family physicians, some pediatricians and internists, and even some medical subspecialists. (I went to a neuroopthalmologist's office just yesterday to see a patient with him.) These practitioners use a new medical model—the biopsychosocial medical model—in their practice. This model is consistent with family systems theory in its focus on multiple levels of the system—from the cell and the individual to the family and the community. These colleagues are our soul mates.

Regardless of whether a patient's health-care provider works from a traditional biomedical or a new biopsychosocial model, therapists and counselors need to work with patients and their families challenged by the onset of a serious illness. The goals of medical family therapy include: (a) helping the family accept the illness and develop a manageable treatment plan, (b) strengthening the patient's healing potential, (c) helping maintain an individual and family identity apart from the illness, (d) opening lines of communication, (e) and resolving old conflicts in new ways.

We get as much as we give in this work. In addition to the personal rewards (which are considerable), there are theoretical gains. Family therapy with ill patients forces the field to reclaim biology, mend the mind–body split, and acknowledge the importance of our physical being and its influence on our emotional and interpersonal lives. Working as part of a health-care team with other health-care providers, even if it is only an occasional case, reminds providers to ask all people who come for therapy about their illness histories, their health beliefs, and their current health status. It is amazing how often behavioral or interpersonal problems are connected with an illness or accident. Perhaps illness functions as a reminder of our mortality; like death, it can cause profound personal and relationship dysfunction if not handled well.

This book is composed of five chapters and an interview by leaders in the field of medical family therapy. The enthusiasm and creativity in these chapters reflect the growing work in this area. Both need and opportunities exist for family therapists who rise to the challenge.

Chapter 1 is a creative and entertaining chapter on what we believe to be the centerpiece of medical family therapy—collaboration with health-care providers. Family therapist Rae Schilling and family physician David Stoller use the words of those working in the field to point the way to surmounting what can be considerable barriers to collaborative practice. Chapter 2 is an interview with my long-time collaborator, Thomas Campbell, who tells us, from the physician's perspective, how to collaborate effectively. Chapter 3 is written by family therapists Jeri Hepworth, William Doherty, and myself; it describes our model of medical family therapy and applies it to the challenges faced by acquired immunodeficiency syndrome (AIDS) patients and their families. Chapter 4, by medical family therapist David Seaburn, discusses somatization and language. Seaburn considers understanding the meaning and metaphor in a patient's physical symptoms. Chapter 5 is by psychologist Michael Gottlieb, who discusses important ethical issues involved in medical family therapy and the chronically ill. The book closes with a thought-provoking chapter by family therapist Donald Williamson (chap. 6), who addresses the links among soma, psyche, and intergenerational family experience.

It is my hope that, with this book, more family therapists will ask their patients (independent of presenting problems) about health issues, past and present, and that some of you will choose to lend your talents directly to the medical teams, health-care settings, and patients in need of your perspective and skills.

—Susan H. McDaniel, PhD

Biographies

S usan H. McDaniel, PhD, is Associate Professor of Psychiatry (Psychology) and Family Medicine at Highland Hospital and the University of Rochester School of Medicine and Dentistry. She is known for her publications in the areas of family therapy supervision and consultation, as well as family systems medicine. She is past Director of the University of Rochester Family Therapy Training Program and current Associate Director of the Division of Family Programs in the Department of Psychiatry, and she co-directs Psychosocial Education in the Department of Family Medicine. Dr. McDaniel is a frequent speaker at national meetings for both disciplines. Dr. McDaniel is on the editorial boards of six journals, the Book Review Editor for *Family Systems Medicine,* and the Associate Editor for Gender Issues for the *Journal of Family Psychotherapy.* She is on the Commission on Accreditation for Marriage and Family Therapy Education, and the AAMFT/STFM Task Force on Family Therapy and Family Medicine. She is the author, with Lyman Wynne and Timothy Weber, of *Systems Consultation* (Guilford Press, 1986); with Thomas Campbell and David Seaburn, of *Family-Oriented Primary Care* (Springer-Verlag, 1990); and with Jeri Hepworth and William Doherty, of *Medical Family Therapy* (Basic Books, 1992).

J on Carlson, PsyD, EdD, is Distinguished Professor at Governors State University in University Park, Illinois, and director of the Lake Geneva, Wisconsin Wellness Clinic. Dr. Carlson has served as the president of the International Association of Marriage and Family Counselors. He has authored 16 books and over 100 professional articles. He serves as the editor of *Individual Psychology: The Journal of Adlerian Theory, Research, and Practice*, as well as *The Family Journal*. He holds a diplomate in Family Psychology from the American Board of Professional Psychology. He is a Fellow of the American Psychological Association, a clinical member of AAMFT, and a certified sex therapist by AASECT. He has received awards for his professional contributions from the American Counseling Association, American Psychological Association, North American Society of Adlerian Psychology, and the International Association of Marriage and Family Counselors. Dr. Carlson and his wife of 25 years, Laura, are the parents of five children.

Contributors

Thomas L. Campbell, MD, is Associate Professor of Family Medicine and Psychiatry at the University of Rochester School of Medicine and Dentistry, Rochester, New York.

William J. Doherty, PhD, is Professor of Family Social Science and Director of the Marriage and Family Therapy Program at the University of Minnesota, St. Paul, Minnesota. He is chair of the Board of Directors of the journal *Family Systems Medicine*, and Co-Director of the Collaborative Family Health Care Coalition.

Michael C. Gottlieb, PhD, practices independently in Dallas, Texas. He is a Diplomate in Family Psychology (ABPP), a Fellow of the American Psychological Association, and an adjunct professor in the Department of Psychology at Texas Woman's University.

Jeri Hepworth, PhD, is Associate Professor and Associate Residency Director in the Department of Family Medicine, University of Connecticut School of Medicine, Hartford, Connecticut.

Rae Schilling, PsyD, is Assistant Professor (CHS) on the faculty of the Eau Claire Family Medicine Residency of the Department of Family Medicine, University of Wisconsin–Madison.

David B. Seaburn, MS, is Assistant Professor of Psychiatry and Family Medicine, University of Rochester School of Medicine and Dentistry, Rochester, New York. He is also Director of the postgraduate Family Therapy Training Program, Department of Psychiatry.

David Stoller, MD, is in private practice in family medicine in Everett, Washington.

Donald S. Williamson, PhD, is senior faculty at the LIOS/Bastyr School of Applied Behavioral Science in Seattle, Washington. He also has a private practice in family psychology.

PART

WORKING WITH
PHYSICIANS

1

Opening the Door to Collaboration with Physicians

Rae J. Schilling, PsyD
David L. Stoller, MD

W hen family therapists join with physicians, new understandings and therapeutic approaches emerge. Collaboration acknowledges that cooperative efforts can bear more fruit than working in isolation. This process of bringing new meaning to old circumstances, through the richness of different perspectives and expectations, is the hallmark of successful medical family therapy. When Engel (1977) proposed the biopsychosocial model for health and illness, one large and obstreperous door blocking collaboration was opened. However, working with physicians can often be an *Alice in Wonderland* experience for family therapists:

> The rabbit-hole went straight on like a tunnel for some way...when suddenly, thump! thump! down she came upon a heap of sticks and dry leaves...before her was another long passage and the White Rabbit was still in sight...she turned the corner...found herself in a long, low hall. There were doors all round the hall, but they were all locked; ...trying every door, she walked sadly down the middle, wondering how she was ever to get out again. (Carroll, 1977, pp. 7–10)

The door to collaboration is now open. Pioneers in this developing field have described the ways to fruitful collaboration with physicians and other medical providers (Doherty & Baird, 1983;

Dym & Berman, 1986; Glenn, 1984, 1985, 1987; Hepworth & Jackson, 1985; Hepworth, Gavazzi, Adlin, & Miller, 1988; Kriesel & Rosenthal, 1986; McDaniel & Campbell, 1986; McDaniel, Hepworth, & Doherty, 1992; Wynne, McDaniel, & Weber, 1987). However, beyond that historic, initial door, many family therapists have found a long, dark hall with many more doors—many of them still closed and locked.

> I have found the door to collaboration locked and bolted. Perhaps you can get it ajar. (Fitzelle, 1992)

> While I see many families dealing with terminal and chronic illness, efforts at collaboration (with physicians) are mostly unsuccessful. (Bergman, 1992)

> Over six years ago, when I first began my private practice, I wrote several area physicians outlining what I believed to be a beneficial collaboration, providing increased attention to contributing, but nonorganic factors of the medical conditions they may be treating. I did not receive any responses. (Lindsley, 1992)

Getting in the door (how to open the door, and what to expect inside) is addressed in the first section of this chapter. Keeping the door open (how to nurture the collaborative relationship) and troubleshooting are addressed in the second section.

Getting in the Door
(The *Alice in Wonderland* Syndrome)

Interest in opening the door to collaboration is an important first step. However, it is just a first step. The hallway you enter may feel quite foreign. For those who are unfamiliar with the medical world, differences in the medical and psychotherapy culture may create a sense of disorientation, confusion, false starts, and miscommunication. As in Wonderland, that which one person may assume to be easily understood may in fact be quite incomprehensible to another.

Understanding the world one is entering may be the key to success. As in joining in any new culture or, for that matter, joining with a new family in therapy, understanding explanatory models, time, language, meaning, and structure makes success in communication more likely. With well-developed understanding of how to assess and join social systems, family therapists are well suited to initiate and facilitate successful collaboration. The following is an overview of the differences therapists should understand before considering specific strategies that are identified for use in opening the next door.

The Cultural Milieu of Medicine

Explanatory Models in Medicine and Family Therapy

> The proponents of competing paradigms...see different things when they look from the same point in the same direction....What cannot even be demonstrated to one group of scientists may seem intuitively obvious to another. (Kuhn, 1970, p. 150)

Medicine and family therapy have been born of divergent schools of thought. Medicine was born of the womb of the reductionist school, which in its purest form believes that everything can be understood by breaking things into smaller and smaller pieces. In its most elemental form, cause and effect are linear. Many of the world-changing biomedical advances of the 20th century have come from this approach. Ecosystemic family therapy was born of the phenomenologic womb. Circular feedback, dynamic hierarchy, and homeostasis inform systemic family therapy. In its purist form, the whole is seen to be more than the sum of its parts.

Although medicine and family therapy do not exist in their primordial forms (they have informed and changed each other), their parental philosophical roots constantly tug at them. Acknowledging and building from those differences is the goal of collaboration. Ransom (1992) noted that "the goal is not to establish new foundations while discarding old ones, but to talk continuously about familiar problems in novel ways until new and useful 'tools' for solving those problems are at hand" (p. 306).

An additional factor to consider is the impact of current health-care trends. With the growing consumer movement, there is a backlash against the medical field for its emphasis on productivity and high-tech progress at the cost of continuity of care and a comprehensive high-touch approach (Naisbitt, 1982). These concerns are pushing physicians to slow down and listen to their patients. At the same time, therapists are experiencing a push in the opposite direction. As health-care costs soar and third-party payers demand more accountability and speed (brief therapy), the therapy field is moving toward greater efficiency. The movement of the two fields toward each other in this way may make it easier to forge effective collaborative relationships.

Society has added yet another level of meaning that can impact collaboration. Medicine, with its scientific methods, focus on the corpus, power, and prestige, has been designated in the collective social construct as *masculine*. Psychotherapy, with its focus on feelings, relationship, and the psyche, has been designated as *feminine*. Cultural and institutional misogyny will no doubt rear its ugly head in the process of collaboration. Regardless of the actual gender, behavior, philosophy, or actions of individual collaborators, the relationship may at times be seen as symbolic of this cultural battle for egalitarianism. In the maturing collaborative relationship, it may be wise to address these issues (e.g., reimbursement differentials, professional roles, and expectations).

Time in Medicine

Phone calls to physicians are the only ones I prepare for. I feel that if I don't make an impact within the first 20 seconds I'm lost. (Smets, 1992)

In March of this year I was asked by the Out-Patient Oncology Unit at the direction of the hospital oncologist (Dr. Z) if I might be able to "visit" with patients while they wait for their treatments and/or see the doctor. The two nurses assigned to the Unit are quite overworked and have little time to sit and really listen to the concerns of patients and families. I have been visiting the Unit for two hours two days a week since March.

Dr. Z has never commented directly to me or to the nurses regarding my presence or interventions. He does request that I remain in the room during his examinations of the patients and frequently points out to me new symptoms and/or aspects of the case that he considers significant. While I believe that he considers my input to be important, I would appreciate some direct feedback from him. However, I have learned from the nurses that he "never stands still long enough" to engage in this type of activity. I am beginning to think that I must assert myself and request that he give me a few minutes to evaluate my role and suggest modifications. (DeVaughn, 1992)

In the medical culture, physicians have learned to "go fast." They are expected to see three to four patients an hour, in contrast to therapists, who see that many patients in half a day. They are taught to "cut to the quick" about what the problem is and how it should be addressed. They are provided with a crew of helpers who are expected to know their work tasks and complete them with a minimum of wasted motion or words. Traditionally, they are expected to take charge quickly and efficiently, and not let emotion "cloud" the equation.

In the family therapy culture, therapists expect to have 45–60 minutes per appointment, and are accustomed to working in isolation. Discussion of clients is rich in descriptive language of affect and relationship and tends to be extensive in scope. Change is expected to occur over a relatively long period of time, with results being primarily subjective. In contrast, the expectation of biomedical intervention is for measurable change by "your next visit"(or sooner). Recognizing, acknowledging, and accepting the different time pressures experienced by each colleague are keys to successful collaboration.

Language and Meaning in Medicine

Just as family therapists have a well-developed style and language, physicians' language is well developed, efficient, and effective in the appropriate context. The following description of one of our patient's medical problems is a good example of effective, efficient medico lingo: "Ms. X was just admitted to the hospital from the ER. She has CHF with orthopnea, paroxysmal nocturnal dyspnea, JVD, hepatomegaly and severe pedal edema. She denies chest pain but her EKG shows new Q waves in the inferior leads and she has bumped her MB fraction to over 40!!" To the physician, this is a rich description of Ms. X's heart attack and the functioning of her failing heart. The uninitiated family therapist may be mystified and misinterpret this as objectification, rather than an attempt to communicate efficiently.

Similarly, the family therapist's language can be equally incomprehensible to the uninitiated physician: "Joey's ED placement is inappropriate because his acting out behaviors are a function of triangulation between the parents in which he is in a cross-generational coalition with Mom in response to Dad's AODA problems." Language is indeed an interactive phenomenon. Successful collaboration requires constant negotiation of effective use of language. If your use of language provokes a response that does not make sense, or if your collaborating physician's language provokes intense response in you, stop and check the language and the meaning, ask questions, and renegotiate. Getting in the door requires clarity of meaning and congruence in mission.

Structure of Medicine

Medicine is organized and compartmentalized; this may help you prioritize your efforts to collaborate and identify areas in medicine that match your interests in family therapy.

Generalist: Specialist: Subspecialist/Primary: Secondary: Tertiary Care. Biopsychosocial theory (Engel, 1977) allows one to imagine a hierarchy of levels of organization for understanding the multiple determinants of health and illness:

> **humanity**
> **nation**
> **culture**
> **community**
> **family**
> **mind–body integration**
> **individual**
> **organ system**
> **organ**
> **tissue**
> **cellular**
> **biochemical**
> **molecular**

The more specialized physicians are, the more likely their focus will be closer to the bottom of the continuum. In contrast, the generalist will begin in the middle and move toward the top, including relevant aspects of the bottom of the continuum. Because of generalists' broader view, they may be more amenable to collaboration than specialists, who do more delegating and referring. Generalists may be less interested in maintaining the mind–body dichotomy and more interested in a systemic view of health and illness. As such, one may find fertile ground for collaboration with generalists.

Primary-care physicians are those who have initial contact with patients. They generally include family physicians, general internists, pediatricians, and occasionally obstetricians/gynecologists. They provide for continuity of care, and act as case managers when referral to secondary and tertiary care (specialist/subspecialist) is necessary (see Table 1.1). Because family physicians focus on broad, multigenerational care, they are most attuned to systemic variables in health and illness. They are also trained in a milieu that includes "behavioral scientists," and so may have some experience with collaboration (Ross & Doherty, 1988; Shapiro, 1980). By the nature of their work, pediatricians must see children in the context of their families. This "systemic setting" makes them good potential collaborators. There is a growing movement among primary-care internists (as opposed to internist specialists) to embrace systemic principles, so they, too, may be potential collaborators.

TABLE 1.1
Structure of Medicine

Category	Generalist	Specialist	Subspecialist
Primary care	Family physician	General internal medicine, pediatrics, obstetrics/gynecology	
Secondary and tertiary care		Internal medicine	Cardiology (heart) Pulmonology (lung) Nephrology (kidney) Rheumatology (joints) Oncology (cancer)
		Psychiatry Pediatrics	Neonatology (newborns) Pediatric cardiology
		General surgery	Cardiovascular (heart and blood vessels) Urology (urinary tract) Ophthalmology (eyes)

This is not to say that all specialists and subspecialists are not interested in collaboration. Rather, their explanatory model is more reductionistic and requires a greater leap to collaboration (as opposed to referral). In contrast, specialists may be more willing to admit that the psychosocial realm is out of their area of expertise, and thus may be eager to collaborate. Those who work in multidisciplinary teams may be particularly good collaborators. Examples may be specialists in rehabilitation medicine, oncologists involved in hospice work, and subspecialists working in specialized chronic illness areas (e.g., hemophilia, cystic fibrosis, sickle cell disease, etc.). With this overview of differences between the two fields, a therapist may want to consider particular strategies for approaching physicians regarding collaboration.

Strategies to Find the Right Door

In our survey of family therapists interested in collaborating with physicians, the following strategies have been successful for some.

1. Those physicians who already refer patients/clients may be interested in considering an even more collaborative relationship. Broach the subject!

2. Those physicians who work well in multidisciplinary teams may have interest and well-developed collaborative skills. Call medical centers or chronic disease-focused agencies (e.g., Spina Bifida Association, Easter Seals, hospices, centers for the developmentally disabled, social service agencies). Libraries will have exhaustive lists for your communities. Then meet with the physicians and the teams.

3. Search out teaching programs in your communities. Residency training programs (postmedical school training programs in large medical centers and in community hospitals), particularly in the primary-care fields, may be fruitful places to begin. Even if there is already a psychologist or counselor on the faculty, new faces are often welcome. Volunteer to provide a 45-minute lecture or a brief workshop for their noon conference series so you can get to know them and they can get to know you. Appropriate topics include: impact of health and illness on families (and vice versa); how to assess for attention deficit disorder (ADD), depression, panic disorders, eating disorders, substance abuse, sexual abuse, and domestic violence; parenting tips to be incorporated in pediatric visits; and physician self-care. Teaching (even as little as a few hours per year) can lead to referrals and ultimately the evolution of closer collaborative relationships.

4. Bass (1992) facilitates collaboration by proxy. She encourages her clients to urge their physicians to collaborate with her, and it works. Suggest that clients let their physicians know that they are in therapy, who their therapist is, what they are working on in therapy, and how it relates to their physical symptoms. For example, a diabetic, single-parent mother of an abusive teenager reported to her physician that her blood sugar levels go out of control each time her son is out of control. Get the client's permission to speak with the physician about how to incorporate the family in symptom management. See McDaniel, Campbell, and Seaburn's (1990) summary of research showing an association of family dysfunction with poor outcome in studies of chronic disease, especially for diabetes.

5. For clients without physicians, refer to physicians who are potential collaborators.

6. Johnson (1992) found propinquity to be a remarkably successful strategy. Rent office space in a physician's office or office building (or vice versa). The availability, frequent contact, and "curbside" consults can parlay into greater collaboration.

Keeping the Door Open

Nurturing the Collaborative Relationship

Once a successful initial link with a physician is established, there are several key guidelines for nurturing the relationship so that collaboration can thrive: (a) be accessible, (b) unshroud the mystery around therapy, and (c) form a personal relationship.

Be Accessible

Family psychologists and counselors typically have therapy arrangements that emphasize privacy to a greater degree than commonly occurs in the medical culture. A private sound-proofed room is considered essential. The provider arranges to be free of phone calls or other interruptions for an extended period for each appointment.

Consider the physician who is accustomed to working in semi-private conditions (e.g., in a clinic room accompanied by an assistant, behind a curtain in a hospital room shared by two or more patients) and who is accustomed to frequent interruptions (e.g., calls from other physicians, an assistant checking on instructions, a pharmacist checking on a drug substitution, etc.). In the interest of efficiency, the physician expects to be interrupted, and similarly expects access to other colleagues.

To make themselves accessible to physician collaborators, therapists can reserve 5–10 minutes on the hour between sessions for receiving or returning calls from referring providers; or they can inform providers that they use 1 hour each day (e.g., 3:00–4:00 p.m.) to take calls from other professionals. For these consultation calls, be brief and to the point. The MD colleague usually does not want all the psychological details; he or she wants to know how he or she can help, and what to expect of the therapist.

At the first visit of a patient referred by a physician, therapists can make a point of getting the patient to sign a release allowing for consultation with the collaborating physician. Better yet, the referring physician could get such consent at the time of referral, so that the therapist is free to let the provider know whether the referred person actually came. Most clients will be open to such arrangements when they know that it means their care will be well coordinated.

Unshroud the Mystery Around Therapy

In the authors' work setting, the counseling records are kept with the patients' medical records. For patients seen in counseling, a family counseling folder is kept with each family's medical chart, which in turn consists of individual family members' charts. At the first consultation visit with a family psychologist or counselor, the patient information packet describes this arrangement. In the 3 years under this arrangement, only one client objected, and that person chose to seek care elsewhere.

Even without the advantage of sharing building space with medical colleagues in the community, therapists can facilitate communication by sending them copies of client records. At a minimum, therapists should send the intake assessment and plan. One of the authors' family counselor colleagues in private practice sends the client's physician a copy of the progress note following each session. This colleague has over 10 years of experience of successful collaboration with physicians.

The previous approach prevents the kind of reaction described by a physician respondent to the collaboration survey. Weiner wrote:

> My major objection to collaboration is how poorly therapists communicate with me. I call a therapist the day I see their client, I send a copy of the history and physical and all progress notes. If I make any type of major intervention I call the therapist immediately. But most of the therapists I work with do not communicate in the same way. I have discussed this many times, but very few therapists cooperate. It is infuriating to me that therapists are in practice to teach clients how to communicate better with their families and themselves, yet they are really setting a poor example for their clients.

Another way to unshroud the mystery is to do joint visits with physicians. Volunteer to be available at the beginning or end of the half day for scheduled joint visits. The therapist could be available to sit in on part of a medical visit. If the medical office has a consultation room, the therapist can offer to conduct the first postreferral session on site at the medical facility so that the physician can sit in on at least part of the visit. Invite a physician to come to the counseling setting for joint sessions. If joint sessions are scheduled at the beginning or end of a half day, some physicians will be glad for the chance to meet the therapist and see the counseling office setting. It is far easier for them to make referrals if they know the therapist and what the patient will encounter when referred.

Form a Personal Relationship

The most rewarding collaboration experiences emerge from the foundation of a personal relationship between the therapist and physician. Susan McDaniel, family therapist and author, offered the following insights regarding her long-term collaboration relationship with family physician, Tom Campbell.

> I really believe it is important for family therapists to connect with as many family physicians as they can, in order to understand and explore the many forms and possibilities that exist for physician-therapist collaboration. However, I also believe that having one stable and close relationship with a physician has been vital to my development as a medical family therapist. Being able to work in depth with Tom has taught me an incredible amount about how physicians work, think, and feel about medicine. He has taught me the language of medicine. We also have a safe enough relationship that I can try out ideas or approaches that I am unsure about and know that he will tell me when there is no way it would fly, and when he thinks I should take a risk. I grew up with a physician as a father and I am married to a physician, so it's not that I am unfamiliar with the territory. But having a close working collaborative relationship has taken me many steps farther in understanding the impact of illness on personal and interpersonal dynamics and understanding how to collaborate with a medical team in providing comprehensive care to patients.

Several of the first author's family therapy colleagues are former behavior science faculty in family medicine residencies. Through their participation in the training of family physicians, they became well acquainted with many of the young doctors coming through the 3-year postmedical school clinical-training component, which directly precedes entry to practice. During the residency training, these doctors sat in on therapy sessions and took advantage of "curbside consults" facilitated by the on-site presence of these behavior scientists. The relationships built through these contacts resulted in numerous referrals over the years, including self-referrals. Physicians who have experienced the benefits of therapy for themselves and their families are an excellent source of therapy referrals. They understand the therapy process and can be helpful in recognizing when a patient could benefit from therapy, letting patients know what to expect from therapy and letting the therapist know what to expect from the patients.

Troubleshooting

Collaboration is sometimes aborted or preceded by painful experiences. McDaniel described one such experience early in her career as a family medicine faculty person:

This experience involved being invited to take an expert role in a faculty development group and then being attacked for doing so. This was a very painful experience for my inexperienced and insecure ego, but it taught me the importance of being peers and respecting the expertise of physicians while sharing the expertise that I have as a therapist. Successful collaboration is a give and take operation, never just giving and also never just taking. I believe therapists must be able to interact with physicians as peers, respecting their strengths while sharing our knowledge.

McDaniel reminds us that any healthy relationship is based on mutual respect, which in turn is based on self-respect (i.e., healthy self-esteem). Had her colleagues been more secure with themselves, it is not likely they would have attacked her. Had she felt more secure, she might have approached them differently with her expertise, or been less bruised by the subsequent attack.

Physician Self-Esteem

Because physicians are so often put on a pedestal, it can be hard to remember that they, too, are human and may suffer from poor self-esteem. Physician self-esteem can become fragile through the long and grueling years of medical education. *The House of God* (Shem, 1981) vividly describes medical training by taking the reader through a year of internship, and describing how several young doctors cope with the hardships endured during that time. Reading this novel can help a therapist understand some of the factors that shape physicians.

McKegney (1989) provided a thought-provoking analysis of similarities between abusive family dynamics and dysfunctional patterns in medical education. Just as understanding how physical or sexual abuse affects clients is helpful in the therapy process, knowing how the medical education system abuses its trainees is helpful in the collaboration process. If the therapist's self-esteem is intact, but the therapist is unaware of how fragile a physician colleague's ego may be, it is all too easy to assume an egalitarian relationship, when, in fact, the prerequisite security of healthy self-esteem is absent in the physician colleague. The imbalance between levels of self-esteem can result in the physician attacking (putting down another to elevate oneself) the therapist colleague. When being attacked for offering expertise, it is easy to become resentful and to feel hurt at the rejection. How can one handle such a situation to everyone's advantage?

In the authors' experience, if, after several attempts to relate on equal footing, both parties are not taking equal responsibility for the health of the relationship, it is not useful to continue to assume peer equality (in terms of secure egos). No matter how much one expects equal responsibility in the relationship, one cannot do it alone. It takes two. Instead, try shifting to a stance that acknowledges the imbalance in responsibility (i.e., when one's colleague is on the attack, he or she is giving away responsibility). Accept that this colleague's level of personal security is insufficient to accept equal responsibility at that moment. Go with the resistance. Use your skills as a therapist and systems thinker. An anonymous therapist's journal excerpt illustrates the processing of such an experience: "By attributing that stance (I'm okay; you are not okay) to me, she is telling me she is not okay. Indirectly, she is telling me, 'Please recognize that I am fragile and please be gentle with me.' So I must be gentle then, as I would with a client or student. It is frustrating to back up to this level when what I seek is a partnership in which both partners carry their own weight."

The dilemma is reminiscent of the dilemma of women who get frustrated with teaching their men how to be equal partners, when what they long for is men who already know how to be equal partners. However, as more and more women have accepted that challenge, more and more men have learned how to be equal partners. Many physician colleagues who are not yet at that level can get there too. Therapists are in a unique position as colleagues to develop "personal" professional relationships with physicians. Those relationships can serve as the foundation for introspection and self-growth among those colleagues.

Therapist Self-Esteem

Because of the power and status differential of physicians over therapists, adequate therapist self-esteem facilitates successful collaboration. The therapist must be secure in what he or she has to offer as a person and a professional. Just as in therapy relationships with clients, the therapist must have the confidence to respond to put-downs of one's person or profession without resorting to attack as a means of defense.

Even in therapy, it is a challenge to respond skillfully to attacks or put-downs. In a therapy relationship, the therapist is more likely to expect (or at least allow for) the other person to be in pain or unenlightened about healthy relationship skills, and thus accept "negative transference" without taking it personally. In collaborating with a professional, it is harder to remember to do the same.

Unless the therapist thinks of him- or herself as an equal with a physician colleague, one is at risk of responding defensively (or is it offensively?) when inadvertent or intentional slights occur. When a physician colleague expects you to interrupt a client session to take his or her call, take that as a colleague who expects the mutual courtesy of quick access, rather than a sign of domination.

How can a therapist best assess whether to continue to give a frustrating physician colleague the benefit of the doubt? As in any other relationship, it is best to express concern directly and assertively. Affirm something about that colleague that is positive despite the frustration, state what is offensive, and specify the preferred behavior. For example:

> I don't like it when you speak to me as if you have the same counseling expertise as I do and you suggest that you simply don't have the time to do it yourself. I want you to acknowledge and respect my special training in this area. I appreciate your interest in psychosocial aspects of health care and encourage you to continue to develop the primary-care counseling skills you have. I also appreciate that you care enough about your patient to recognize your limitations (be they time or skill level) and take the trouble to set up this referral.

The response given to this type of approach will help the therapist determine how much to invest in the particular relationship. If the physician colleague acknowledges and validates the concern, even if not immediately, the relationship probably has good potential. When the physician seems unable or unwilling to respond in ways that the therapist needs or wants, the therapist should not keep filling a bottomless bucket. When the investment is consistently and significantly greater than the returns, and there are no signs of change apparent, the therapist can best move on to other medical colleagues.

Painful experiences are not inherent in collaboration. What distinguishes rewarding collaboration from painful collaboration? Perhaps the answer lies in the stance of the therapist seeking collaboration. de Shazer (1984) emphasized that resistance is in the eye of the beholder. Therapists learn to recognize that if clients "won't" do what the former expect, it may mean that the therapists are asking the latter to do more than they are able to do with their current knowledge and skills. The same applies to colleagues.

Psychologist Smets gave the following example, in which a problematic referral situation was resolved. Rather than becoming angry at the physician for not meeting his expectations, he identified the missing knowledge and skills and offered assistance:

A local pediatrician was prescribing counseling as a prerequisite for dispensing Ritalin prescriptions for children with Attention Deficit Hyperactivity Disorder. Because of her medical model, doctor-centered approach in which she ordered the parents to take their children to counseling, I encountered one hostile parent after another coming in because they were "forced to by the doctor." I spoke with her about using a more patient-centered dialogue rather than prescriptive approach. "Doctor, I admire your approach to ADD patients. You are not taking the easy way out by simply prescribing Ritalin as so many other physicians do. I am impressed that you understand the importance of education and other factors such that you make the effort to insist on combining the medication prescription with a therapy prescription. One thing you may not realize is that some patients have been responding negatively to your well-informed therapy referrals. In part, these reactions are because there is still a stigma associated with psychological services. Another factor is that psychological services are not always reimbursed as well as medical services. Usually there is only partial coverage and sometimes none at all. I recommend that you check the patient's level of readiness to accept a referral. Sometimes just talking about it lowers the threshold or pinpoints barriers that can be overcome once identified. If I can help with any of those barriers, please let me know."

The pediatrician was responsive to my suggestions and the people referred are now much more receptive to the services for which they were sent. On the basis of that positive experience, he also approached her about his concern regarding Ritalin prescriptions. She would prescribe Ritalin to be taken twice a day on school days and not at all on weekends. His preference was to use a Ritalin trial as part of the assessment process. I explained that having the child initially take it three times a day and on weekends provides the opportunity for feedback from home as well as school regarding what effect the medication might have. The physician now collaborates in this approach. Once educated about how the Ritalin is affecting the presenting problem, she changed the prescription as needed.

Knowing and valuing oneself, and communicating clearly and openly about differences with one's collaborator, will facilitate mutual respect and encourage the richness of difference that collaboration brings. Collaboration is not the process of conversion, but the development of new meanings by and for all parties involved.

Conclusion

Initially collaboration can feel like a free-fall down the Rabbit's hole. However, bringing together the expertise of therapist and physician can facilitate new understanding and innovation in the care of our clients. Collaboration can occur on many levels. Depending on the needs of therapist, physician, and clients/patients, collaboration can move fluidly between:

referral <—> consultation <—> conjoint therapy.

As in any professional relationship, collaboration will require active introspection, communication, and exploration in an environment of mutual respect and openness. Although challenging, it is an adventure that is desirable, enjoyable, and productive.

References

Carroll L. (1977). *Alice's adventure in wonderland.* Norwalk, CT: Easton Press.

de Shazer, S. (1984). The death of resistance. *Family Process, 23,* 11–17.

Doherty, W. J., & Baird M. A. (1983). *Family therapy and family medicine: Toward the primary care of families.* New York: Guilford.

Dym B., & Berman, S. (1986). The primary health care team: Family physician and family therapist in joint practice. *Family Systems Medicine, 4,* 9–21.

Engel, G. L. (1977). The need for a new medical model: A challenge for biomedicine. *Science, 196*(4286), 129–136.

Glenn, M. L. (1984). Integrating a family therapist into a family medical practice. *Family Systems Medicine, 2,* 137-145.

Glenn, M. L. (1985). Toward collaborative family-oriented health care. *Family Systems Medicine, 3,* 466–475.

Glenn, M. L. (1987). *Collaborative health care.* New York: Praeger.

Hepworth, J., & Jackson, M. (1985). Health care for families: Models of collaboration between family therapists and family physicians. *Family Relations, 34,* 123–127.

Hepworth, J., Gavazzi, S., Adlin, M., & Miller, W., (1988). Training for collaboration: Internships for family therapy students in a medical setting. *Family Systems Medicine, 6,* 69–79.

Kriesel, H. T., & Rosenthal, D. M. (1986). The family therapist and the family physicians: A cooperative model. *Family Medicine, 18,* 197–200.

Kuhn, T. S. (1970). *The structure of scientific revolutions.* Chicago: University of Chicago Press.

McDaniel, S. H., & Campbell, T. L. (1986). Physicians and family therapists: The risk of collaboration. *Family Systems Medicine, 4,* 25–30.

McDaniel, S. H., Campbell, T. L., & Seaburn, D. (1990). *Family-oriented primary care: A manual for physicians.* New York: Springer-Verlag.

McDaniel, S. H., Hepworth, & J., Seaburn, D. (1990). *Family-oriented primary care: A manual for medical providers.* New York: Springer-Verlag.

McDaniel, S. H., Hepworth, J., & Doherty, W. (1992). *Collaboration with medical providers: Medical family therapy*. New York: Basic Books.

McKegney, C. P. (1989). Medical education: A neglectful and abusive family system. *Family Medicine, 21*(6), 452–457.

Naisbitt, J. (1982). *Megatrends: Ten new directive transforming our lives*. New York: Warner Books.

Ransom, D.C. (1992). Yes, there is a future for behavioral scientists in academic family medicine. *Family Systems Medicine, 10*(3), 305–315.

Ross, J. L., & Doherty, W. J. (1988). Systems analysis and guidelines for behavioral scientists in family medicine. *Family Medicine, (1)*, 46–50.

Shapiro, J. (1980). A revisionist theory for the integration of behavioral science into family medicine. *The Journal of Family Practice, 10*(2), 275–282.

Shem, S. (1981). *The house of God*. New York: Dell.

Wynne, L. C., McDaniel, S. H., & Weber, T. (1987). *Systems consultation: A new perspective for family therapy*. New York: Guilford.

■ ■ ■

2

Collaboration Between Family Therapists and Physicians
An Interview with Thomas L. Campbell, MD

Susan H. McDaniel, PhD

Tom Campbell is a family physician with both medical–psychiatric liaison training and family therapy training. He and I have worked together since 1983 teaching, writing, and seeing patients. The following are his thoughts about psychologists collaborating with physicians.

Susan: Tom, physicians seem to prefer working on their own. What drew you to collaborate with family therapists?

Tom: Well, Susan, early in my training, I became interested in the psychosocial aspects of medical care, and began counseling some of my patients. The more patients I counseled, the more I realized that I didn't have adequate time or skills, even with advanced fellowship training, to deal with many of the psychosocial problems that my patients had. So, I started to look around for help; both to learn more about family systems, and for therapists to whom I could refer my more challenging patients.

Susan: You're a family physician, a primary-care doctor. Could you educate us a little bit about what family physicians do?

Tom: Family physicians provide primary medical care for entire families, and therefore include parts of pediatrics, obstetrics/gynecology, internal medicine, psychology, and other specialties. By *primary care* I mean physicians who provide comprehensive and continuous care for all types of medical problems. Family practice is based on a biopsychosocial approach to health care, in which patients are evaluated in their psychosocial contexts, and psychosocial problems sometimes take on equal importance with medical problems. This approach is particularly relevant because a good deal of research has shown that most mental health problems are cared for exclusively in the nonpsychiatrist medical system and are never seen by mental health specialists. The primary medical systems have been called the de facto mental health-care system for the United States. Thus, additional training in the recognition and treatment of mental health problems is particularly important for primary-care physicians.

Susan: That's very interesting. I thought that this was our territory, but it's clear that you all are doing as much or more of it than we therapists are. Can you tell us something about what the focus of your own work is right now?

Tom: My primary interest is to better understand what role the family should play in the medical practice, from clinical teaching and research perspectives. Clinically, I am trying to develop and put into practice my own approach to what has been called *family systems medicine*, which is an integration of family therapy, systems theory, and medical practice. In our teaching, as you know, we have been trying to help family practice residents to integrate the family into primary care. Our book, written with David Seaburn, *Family-Oriented Primary Care* is a practical manual on how to do this. In the area of research, I have reviewed the literature that demonstrates that families have a powerful influence on physical health. The National Institute of Mental Health published this work as a book entitled *Families' Impact on Health*. In addition, I write a regular column in the journal *Family Systems Medicine*, called "Research Reports." I am also working on a collaborative research project in our department examining how family relationships influence cardiovascular disease.

Susan: Let me shift our conversation a bit now. Tom, why do you think physicians have the reputation with therapists of being difficult to work with and uninterested in psychological and family issues?

Tom: Well, I think many therapists hold this stereotype of physicians. It is important to recognize that physicians do live in a very different culture than mental health providers. We receive very different training, use a different language, and operate with very different theoretical models. For example, one important value for many physicians is that physical health is more important than mental health and, therefore, takes priority over it. Physicians have many similar stereotypes of therapists—that they are difficult to work with and uninterested in physical health problems. Both of these views result from having two different cultures and a lack of interaction between our disciplines.

Susan: Let me ask you for some advice then. How can a family therapist get over feeling intimidated by the medical system? What would you say to someone who wants to work more with medical providers? How does one get started?

Tom: Probably the first step is to get to know a physician on a one-to-one basis and use that relationship as an entry into the medical system. There are a couple of ways one can do that. One is to contact the physician of one of the patients, or *clients* as you call them, that you are seeing, preferably a physician who seems to be particularly interested in psychosocial and mental health problems. Have lunch with him or her. I would begin by discussing areas of common interest. Tell him or her about your areas of specialty, and ask about what kinds of psychosocial problems he or she sees most frequently. Of those, which does he or she refer? Which kinds of patients does he or she find most worrying or frustrating? You might also consult with the physicians of clients who have medical problems to learn more about those problems and how they impact on your client. Another suggestion is to contact your own physician and talk with him or her about how you might get more involved with the health-care system. Once you get a foot in the door, there are usually opportunities to collaborate with health-care providers and consult for hospitals or other kinds of treatment systems.

Susan: Okay, let's assume that as a therapist I have gotten a referral from a physician. Now what do I do? What is it that most physicians want from a family therapist, and how can I be sure to maintain a good collaborative relationship?

Tom: That will vary a lot depending on the physician and the specific consultation. Probably the safest thing to do is ask the physician what it is that he or she wants from you. For some cases, and with some physicians, this initial letter of referral and a summary letter at the end of treatment are all that are wanted. With other more complex cases, the physician may want ongoing phone conversations about the progress of therapy. Most physicians will want to know if there are any significant changes that may impact on medical care. Sometimes a physician will refer a patient or family that he or she is having difficulty working with. In these cases, it is particularly important to get the physician involved in the treatment process to explore the difficulties. I would also recommend inviting the physician to do the first visit with any referral. Most of the time the physician will not come, but in some cases he or she will, and that can be invaluable. For patients who have significant health problems or physical complaints related to the reason for the referral, I encourage therapists to go to the physician's office to see the patient with the physician for the first visit. This is often one of the few ways that you can join with these patients and engage them in history.

Susan: Well, thank you very much. It actually sounds doable when you describe it like that. Is there anything else that would be helpful for family psychologists to know about collaborating with physicians like you?

Tom: I would say the single most important principle is for therapists to use the same systems principles used with patients and clients in working with physicians and other health-care providers. By that I mean therapists should try to understand the physician's own context and the health-care system, and view the referral process as a collaborative relationship between professionals from different cultures, in which both parties contribute equally to its success or failure. This will help prevent therapists from blaming the medical system, or "doctor-bashing," when things don't go as smoothly as they could. I also think it is important to recognize how much therapists have to offer to physicians and the medical care system. Physicians care for many patients with significant mental health and relationship problems. These problems often masquerade as medical problems, such as noncompliance or difficulty changing health behaviors. Most physicians will be quite open and receptive to working collaboratively with mental health providers once they trust you and see that you have something to offer.

Susan: Well, thank you very much. Is there any literature on collaboration you could recommend?

Tom: I have the bibliography that we have developed together, and I will highlight two books. One is *Family-Oriented Primary Care*, which addresses collaboration from the physician perspective; the other is *Medical Family Therapy*, which is written for the family therapist and has a chapter on collaboration with medical providers. Why don't we include the entire bibliography so that your readers can access as much of this information as they would like?

Bibliography

Candib, L., & Glenn, M. (1983). Family medicine and family therapy: Comparative development, methods, and roles. *Journal of Family Practice, 16*(4), 773–779.

Cole-Kelly, K., & Hepworth, J. (1991). Performance pressures: Saner responses for consultant family therapists. *Family Systems Medicine, 9*, 159–164.

Crane, D.D. (1986). The family therapist, the primary care physician and the Health Maintenance Organization: Pitfalls and possibilities. *Family Systems Medicine, 4*, 22–30.

Doherty,W.J., & Baird, M.A. (1986). Developmental levels in family centered medical care. *Family Medicine, 18*, 153–156.

Doherty, W.J., & Baird, M.A. (Eds.). (1987). *Case studies in family centered medical care.* New York: Guilford.

Doherty, W.J., & Campbell, T.L. (1988). *Families and health.* Beverly Hills, CA: Sage.

Dym, B., & Berman, S. (1986). The primary health care team: Family physician and family therapist in joint practice. *Family Systems Medicine, 4*, 9–21.

Glenn, M.L. (1984). Integrating a family therapist into a family medical practice. *Family Systems Medicine, 2*, 137–145.

Glenn, M.L. (1985). Toward collaborative family-oriented health care. *Family Systems Medicine, 3*, 466–475.

Glenn, M.L. (1987). *Collaborative health care.* New York: Praeger.

Hepworth, J., Gavazzi, S., Adlin, M., & Miller, W. (1988).Training for collaboration: Internships for family therapy students in a medical setting. *Family Systems Medicine, 6*, 69–79.

Hepworth, J., & Jackson, M. (1986). Health care for families: Models of collaboration between family therapists and family physicians. *Family Relations, 34*, 123–127.

Huygen, F.J.A. (1982). *Family medicine: The medical life history of families.* New York: Brunner/Mazel.

Kriesel, H.T., & Rosenthal., D.M. (1986). The family therapist and the family physician: A cooperative model. *Family Medicine, 18*, 197–200.

McCall, C., & Storm, C.L. (1985). Family therapists and family therapy programs in hospital programs: A survey. *Family Systems Medicine, 3*, 143–150.

McDaniel, S.H. (1992). Implementing the biopsychosocial model: The future for psychosocial specialists. *Family Systems Medicine, 10*, 277–281.

McDaniel, S.H., & Amos, S. (1983). The risk of change: Teaching family as the unit of medical care. *Family Systems Medicine, 1*(3), 25–30.

McDaniel, S.H., & Campbell, T.L. (1986). Physicians and family therapists: The risk of collaboration. *Family Systems Medicine, 4*, 4–8.

McDaniel, S.H., Campbell, T.L., & Seaburn, D. (1990). *Family-oriented primary care: A manual for physicians.* New York: Springer-Verlag.

McDaniel, S.H., Hepworth, J., & Doherty, W. (1992). *Collaboration with medical providers. Medical family therapy.* New York: Basic Books.

Medalie, J.H., & Cole-Kelly, K. (1993). Behavioral science and family medicine collaboration: A developmental paradigm. *Family Systems Medicine, 11*, 15–23.

Ransom, D.C. (1992). Yes, there is a future for behavioral scientists in academic family medicine. *Family Systems Medicine, 10*, 305–315.

Sargent, J. (1985). Physician-family therapist collaboration: Children with medical problems. *Family Systems Medicine, 3*, 454–465.

Seaburn, D.B., Gawinski, B.A., Harp, J., McDaniel, S.H., Waxman, D., & Shields, C. (1993). Family systems therapy in a primary care medical setting: The Rochester experience. *Journal of Marital & Family Therapy, 19*(2), 177–190.

Wood, B.L. (1995). A developmental biopsychosocial approach to the treatment of chronic illness in children. In R. Mikesell, D. Lusterman, & S. McDaniel (Eds.), *Family psychology and systems therapy: A handbook.* Washington, DC: American Psychology Association Press.

Wynne, L.C., McDaniel, S.H., & Weber, T. (1987). *Systems consultation: A new perspective for family therapy.* New York: Guilford.

PART

MEDICAL FAMILY THERAPY WITH SPECIFIC PROBLEMS

3

Families and AIDS: The Medical Family Therapy Approach

Jeri Hepworth, PhD
Susan H. McDaniel, PhD
William J. Doherty, PhD

I have so much anger and hate for this illness. It is taking my daughter from me, and there is nothing I can do to stop it. Some days she wants me near, and other days she wants me to leave. I think she doesn't want me to see her die...and I am jealous of mothers who have healthy children. (Ava Miro[1], a patient whose 23-year-old daughter is sick with acquired immunodeficiency syndrome [AIDS]).

As the incidence of AIDS increases, our counseling and therapy practices will include more patients with AIDS and families like the Miros. Families of persons with AIDS (PWA) represent all economic, social, and ethnic groups, but all live with the uncertainty and social stigma of AIDS. All try to cope with the frightening illness of someone close to them. When they come to our offices, the family members may be cousins or siblings of people with AIDS.

---

[1] Ava Miro (not her real name) has given permission for her quote to be used.

They do not provide much direct care for the ill person, but wonder why they are feeling depressed, anxious, or stressed. Other clients are parents who live far from their young adult children who have been diagnosed with human immunodeficiency virus (HIV) infection. Still others are family members—lovers, grandmothers, parents, former spouses, or children—who come specifically for support as they cope with the daily concerns of someone who has AIDS.

At present, particular therapists become recognized for their work with PWAs, keep up with the voluminous literature about psychosocial aspects of AIDS, and provide the majority of psychosocial care. But this arrangement of psychotherapeutic specialization for families with AIDS cannot continue. Each patient with AIDS is surrounded by family and friends, and there are increasing numbers of patients. By the end of 1992, more than 250,000 people in the United States had been diagnosed with AIDS (Centers for Disease Control and Prevention, 1992), with nearly 50,000 people diagnosed during 1992. Thus, all therapists must be prepared to treat families that cope with the medical, ethical, financial, social, and psychological effects of HIV-related illness.

This chapter describes medical family therapy for patients and families living with these concerns. First, we describe the fundamentals of the medical family therapy approach. Then we identify some of the central family issues surrounding AIDS, and examine the Miro family's experience to consider how therapists can enhance the overall treatment of patients and families.

Medical Family Therapy

Medical family therapy is a systems approach to psychotherapy with patients and families experiencing a medical illness, trauma, or disability (McDaniel, Hepworth, & Doherty, 1992). This approach assumes that no biomedical event occurs without psychosocial repercussions, and that no psychosocial event occurs without some biological feature. Medical family therapy recognizes that a patient has an illness, that families are affected by illness, and that patient care is influenced by emotional responses and family dynamics. A comprehensive approach to biopsychosocial problems, like AIDS, requires collaboration among medical providers, medical family therapists, and families.

The recent development of medical family therapy is consistent with original conceptualizations of family therapy as a systems approach to mental and physical health. Pioneers such as Auerswald,

Bowen, Minuchin, and Wynne expressed an early commitment to integrated physical and mental health-care treatment. However, their convictions did not become widespread among family therapists. Mainstream family therapy defined itself in opposition to the paternalistic, biologically focused orientation of the traditional Western medical model. In the meantime, some areas within medicine, particularly the discipline of family medicine, have been influenced by physician Engel's (1977) biopsychosocial model. Engel proposed that health care includes attention to all systems, including cells, organ systems, the individual, and the family and social contexts.

Since the early 1980s, systems-oriented medical providers and family therapists have worked together in medical offices and training centers, developed the field of family systems medicine (Bloch, 1983; Ransom, 1983), and explored the application of family systems concepts to medical practice (Doherty & Baird, 1983; McDaniel, Campbell, & Seaburn, 1990). As of 1993, there exists an established literature, a journal, *Family Systems Medicine*, books, and professional meetings that focus on exciting applications of collaborative family-oriented care.

Medical family therapy uses a biopsychosocial systems theory (Doherty, Baird, & Becker, 1987) to help families attend to the effects of illness on their emotional lives and family dynamics. Goals for medical family therapy include: better coping with a chronic illness, enhanced communication about illness and care within the family and with health providers, negotiation of management plans and ways to share care, help for making a lifestyle change, and greater acceptance of a physical problem that cannot be cured. For a family coping with AIDS, specific goals might include: enhancing family communication, deciding how to communicate with others about the illness, negotiating care for the increasing ill patient, planning the extent of medical intervention, and increasing pleasure with life for the patient and the family.

Overarching goals of all medical family therapy are the promotion of *agency* and *communion* (McDaniel et al., 1992).[2] *Agency* describes a family's sense that it makes choices and manages the illness and other aspects of its lives. *Communion* refers to the family's communication and its emotional connections both within and outside the family. Agency and communion often become frayed by the demands and isolation that accompany severe illness and disability.

---

[2] These terms were first used in a discussion of theology and psychology by Bakan (1969).

Unhappily, AIDS exemplifies this pattern because there are high demands on caregivers, a sense of control is diminished, and the illness is often associated with secrecy, denial, and isolation.

HIV and AIDS: Epidemiology and Cultural Response

Since its recognition only a decade ago, AIDS has become a public health issue and an education concern, and has acquired strong cultural and emotional meanings. Along with the overwhelming amount of lay information about AIDS, epidemiologists at the Centers for Disease Control and Prevention (CDC) in Atlanta have carefully monitored transmission and disease progression of AIDS, providing more accurate statistics than for almost any other disease. All cases of AIDS must be reported to state public health departments, however, there is no mandated reporting of those infected with HIV but not diagnosed with AIDS. Thus, we have no accurate estimate of how many thousands of Americans are infected with HIV.

Until 1992, people moved from a diagnosis of HIV positive to AIDS only after they had contracted one of the potentially fatal opportunistic infections, such as pneumocystis carini pneumonia, or Kaposi's sarcoma. The past few years have brought medical advances, including the development of AZT and DDI—drugs that postpone opportunistic infections and increase the life span of many with AIDS. In 1992, the CDC expanded the case definition for AIDS to better identify those with severe HIV infection who might benefit from early medical treatment. Diagnosis of AIDS requires HIV infection plus an opportunistic infection, or when a measure of immune system functioning, the CD4 (helper T-lymphocyte cell count), falls below 200 cells per microliter of blood (normal T-cell count is around 1,000).

The CDC estimate that the new definition will increase the number of people defined as having AIDS by as much as 40%. Increasing the number of persons defined with AIDS who have not developed opportunistic infections also decreases the fatality rate. Thus, in the 1990s, more patients appear to live longer after their diagnosis with AIDS.

In the mid-1980s, people with AIDS were expected to die within 2 or 3 years after diagnosis. In research on physical and psychological variables related to survival, long-term survivors of AIDS were defined by living at least 3 years postdiagnosis. In 1987, Solomon and Temoshok found that expectation of 5-year survival was only 15%. But with AZT (available since 1986), other experimental drugs, enhanced medical treatments for infections, earlier identification of HIV infection, and dietary and lifestyle changes to reduce stress and illness susceptibility, people now are actually living longer with AIDS.

Our cultural response to AIDS is mediated by and reflected in our language. This disease grabs our attention with a label of capitalized initials—HIV and AIDS—rather than more accustomed words like cancer, diabetes, or even tuberculosis. We try to draw lines about AIDS, such as the distinction between HIV and AIDS, or between risky and safer sexual behaviors. Many want to make distinctions between the kinds of people who get AIDS and those who do not. The distinctions may be attempts to find security in the face of a frightening epidemic. Yet the distinctions cannot be clear. The disease spectrum is a continuum—there are degrees of safer sexual behavior, and one cannot observe who is or will be infected with HIV.

Societal attempts to make distinctions lead to discrimination between groups, and result in discrimination in the social and political sense that we recognize. Without acknowledging the natural tendency to find distinctions, and to discriminate the safe from the unsafe, we cannot help patients and families with AIDS cope with the discrimination with which they live.

The opportunistic infections resulting from the impaired immune systems of persons with AIDS are described as attacking, goal-oriented, invading diseases. Unlike most forms of cancer, and almost any other disease, AIDS has associated images of personal culpability, if not punishment. The power of these covert meanings becomes apparent in the family and societal responses to persons diagnosed with these illnesses. To provide more than superficial support, medical family therapists must consider the cultural meanings of the illness, unique family explanatory models, and cultural hesitancies about dealing with death when working with patients and families with AIDS.

HIV and AIDS: Family Responses

Rolland (1984) described how family responses differ by developmental phases of illness, much like developmental stages of families. Rolland suggested concerns and family tasks for each of the crisis, chronic, and terminal phases of illness. In an article on families and AIDS, Rait (1991) suggested alternative wording for the illness stages: *acute, chronic,* and *resolution.* These terms convey the continuum of family experiences and responsibilities associated with patients with AIDS.

Generally in the *acute phase*, the patient, and sometimes the family, learns of the HIV diagnosis, but symptoms of AIDS are not present. During the acute phase, the patient is tested for HIV, and the family begins to address the issues of stigma, fear, disclosure, and early recognition of untimely death.

Walker's (1991) comprehensive book about AIDS and families, *In the Midst of Winter*, includes an extensive chapter about the complexities of HIV testing and disclosure. Testing centers often require that people obtain pre- and posttest counseling to assess their readiness for hearing a diagnosis, and to discuss their initial plans, beliefs, and support systems. People who are diagnosed with HIV are encouraged to share their diagnosis with someone, at which point families become affected.

Treatment must recognize each family's special context, including the social demographic characteristics and attitudes about illnesses. AIDS disproportionately affects families that are African American, Latino, and economically disadvantaged (Centers for Disease Control and Prevention, 1991). Although transmission of HIV by heterosexual contact continues to increase, persons with AIDS often are presumed to be lesbians and gay men or intravenous (IV) drug users. When lesbians and gay men or IV drug users are diagnosed with AIDS, their family members may learn both of the AIDS and of the hidden behavior. Because these behaviors are often disparaged, families can adopt cultural perceptions that make them less accepting of their family member with AIDS. Whatever the mode of transmission, people with AIDS can be subtly or overtly blamed for their illness, and the stigma, shame, and secrecy become a family concern.

Even when families readily accept their family member with AIDS, they worry about how others will respond, and often keep their member's diagnosis a secret. Families make decisions about who is close enough to be a confidant. At work, lovers have to pretend that "a good friend is sick," rather than receive support because their partner is dying. Parents sometimes struggle with how to include their son's lover in their family rituals during their son's illness and death. Some hospitals have changed their policies about allowing only close family members to visit when a patient is in the intensive care unit, reflecting recognition of various family and friendship networks. Yet many families need support for negotiating these new relationships among themselves and with others. It is here that the role for medical family therapists can be crucial.

During the *chronic phase*, the HIV patient becomes increasingly sick with AIDS symptoms. During this time, the patient's family manages to care for the ill person; await any new medical crisis; and cope with the administrative, financial, and social burdens of someone with a chronic or long-term illness. It is physically tiring and emotionally exhausting work to negotiate physical and medical care, adapt to changing family roles, and "try to live a normal life in abnormal conditions" (Rolland, 1988).

During the *phase of resolution*, the patient and family recognize the significant deterioration of health as a signal of impending death. The patient and family ideally use this time to connect more meaningfully with one another, clarify wishes for final medical care, arrange ways to share patient care so that all family members feel included, and all have opportunities to say good-bye.

It is fortunate when families have the opportunity and the time frame for some resolution of family relationships. Often there is not sufficient time, and a patient dies after a brief illness with many unfinished family concerns. Another unfortunate pattern with AIDS is that the patient and family may be able to say good-bye, are as ready as possible for the patient's death, and the patient recovers from the particular infection. We know families that have gone through this grueling process more than once, and are filled with ambivalent and guilty feelings when they are pleased that the person is alive, at the same time that they want the entire process to be over.

The therapist can be helpful throughout the period of resolution—during the end stages of the patient's illness, during the acute bereavement period, and in the months following death. Sometimes when patients are dying, they no longer want to talk with therapists, or with all of their relatives. Families may experience this as rejection, rather than understanding it as a way to cope. One man, dying from AIDS, explained to his siblings that he just could not keep saying good-bye to them; he met with each of them separately, and for the last 10 days of his life asked only to spend time with his long-term lover. Families can use therapeutic support during this transition time.

These family issues become less abstract when considered for a particular family. The Miro family is a family that has been coping with AIDS for more than 3 years. Different family members, and the family as a whole, have been seen by a medical family therapist at different times for more than 2 years. Medical family therapy techniques have been useful for helping them achieve their goals of communicating and caring for one another, becoming closer to one another, increasing their sense of control around medical and life decisions, and living fuller lives as one of their family members lives with AIDS.

The Miro family, whose genogram is available in Fig. 3.1, is a family that has coped with multiple stresses surrounding AIDS.

Valerie Miro was a 21-year-old married woman and mother who became gravely ill immediately following the birth of her second child. Diagnosed with pneumocystic pneumonia, Valerie was in a coma for 3 days and placed on a respirator. Her acute illness was her first signal that she was HIV positive and had AIDS, and her family remained in the hospital praying for her recovery.

Valerie lived with her husband, Juan, in an apartment across the street from her mother, stepfather, and brother, Miguel. Her father also lived in the same city, and all family members provided significant support to one another. Two years prior to the birth, Valerie and Juan had separated, and Valerie had moved to another city and had a sexual relationship with a man, whom she later learned was HIV positive. Valerie and Juan reunited, and Louisa was conceived as a statement of their recommitment.

The shock of the diagnosis and severity of Valerie's illness placed significant burdens on the family. The new baby, who was to represent the family's future, instead became associated with illness, anticipated death, and a reminder of the couple's separation. Overnight, Valerie moved from a healthy young woman to someone who required regular and careful medical attention, Juan and Louisa required HIV testing, and all family members had feelings of unfairness, fury, and sadness. Ava, Valerie's mother, described her feelings to her family physician, who referred her to a medical family therapist.

Early in the family's treatment, Valerie refused therapy. Occasionally, Ava's husband or son attended, but therapy generally focused on Ava's adaptation to her daughter's illness, her own increased responsibilities with her grandchildren, and the impact of the impending loss on her other relationships. From Ava's perspective, Valerie did not care for herself adequately. In addition to refusing therapy, Valerie missed medical appointments, often missed taking her medication, and enjoyed staying out late dancing and drinking. After a year, Valerie had her second bout of pneumocystis, was hospitalized for 3 weeks, and asked to see the medical family therapist.

During two or three hospital visits, Valerie described her fear, decided to take her medication and have her husband use condoms,

FIG. 3.1. Miro family genogram

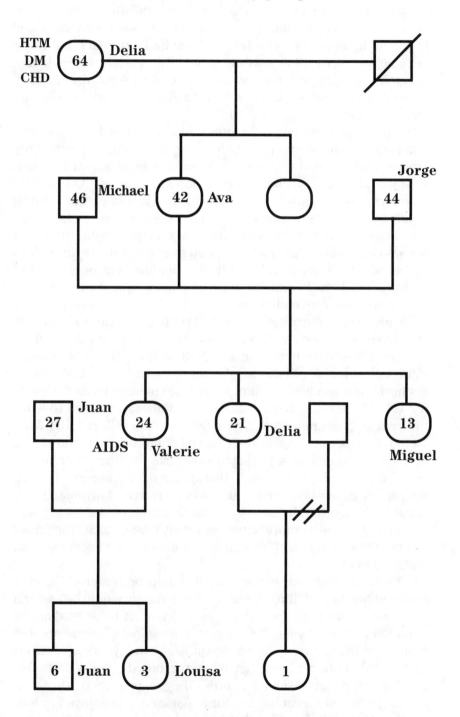

but also described her belief that she would get well if she did not act as if she were sick. After discharge, Valerie attended a few sessions—alone, with her mother, and with her husband, who had tested negative. In an individual session, she stated her belief that if she became sick her husband would leave. She agreed to include him in a joint meeting, but then stopped attending sessions. She telephoned to say that she did not want to discuss this right now, and wanted to stop therapy for a while.

Throughout this time, her mother, Ava, continued with therapy. Ava increased her responsibility for the grandchildren, particularly Louisa, and decided that she could no longer maintain her part-time job. During this time, Valerie stopped taking her AZT, and refused to allow her doctor to talk with her family or the medical family therapist. As Ava took on more concrete responsibilities, she also began to realize that she could not change her daughter, and became less preoccupied with her daughter's health. As difficult as it was to watch her daughter's health decline, Ava began to feel better about herself, and felt support from her husband, Valerie's father, and other extended family.

Nearly 2 years after diagnosis, a third serious medical crisis brought Valerie back to therapy. Although she still would not take medication, she allowed the physician and medical family therapist to share information, and she began to take better care of herself. She asked her husband about his commitment, and he volunteered that he could not tolerate her illness, had started an affair, and wanted to leave the marriage, but remain an active father to the children. Her fears were justified, but she also felt that she could finally acknowledge and cope with her illness. During this last year, Valerie and her mother have had individual and family therapy, and Valerie cares for herself, although her health continues to deteriorate. Fortunately, her daughter has tested HIV negative. Valerie now appreciates her self-sufficiency, but also appreciates her family's assistance. The family has made plans for the future, and has also enjoyed some special family activities.

This is not a dream come true. It would be easier if Valerie's husband had been willing to stay, and it certainly would be easier if there was more hope for Valerie. Her physician believes that she will die in the next year. Yet given that prognosis, Valerie and her family are living a fuller, more joyful life than 2 years ago. Ava is very sad that she will lose her daughter, but she and Valerie feel that they truly have each other now. They respect each other's autonomy, and call on each other for assistance. Ava enjoys her husband and son, relationships that previously had been deteriorating.

Valerie has learned to work with her illness, to monitor her symptoms and activities, and moves between an awareness of impending death and an active appreciation of life.

As we examine this case in retrospect, there might have been better ways for Valerie to encourage her husband's involvement at an earlier time in her illness. This might have decreased the likelihood that he would leave the marriage. However, given Juan's own early family-of-origin experiences, it may be that no extra support could help him tolerate watching his wife's health decline. The relationship between Valerie and her mother was a central supporting relationship, but Valerie also felt much support from her own father, Jorge, and from her stepfather, Michael. Perhaps the presence of these supportive fathers and grandfathers enabled the end of the marriage to be less traumatic than it might have been.

Medical family therapy with a chronic illness like AIDS is ongoing, flexible treatment. Exemplified by this case, different combinations of family members may attend sessions, individual work may be included with family work, and sessions may be frequent during one period and occasional during others. The following clinical strategies are presented to guide treatment with families like the Miros.

Medical Family Therapy Strategies for Families Dealing with AIDS

Respect Defenses, Remove Blame, and Accept Unacceptable Feelings

Families with chronic illness want to know why an illness occurred and who or what is at fault. With AIDS, this search for blame is culturally sanctioned. Indeed, we often inquire about the mode of transmission for persons diagnosed with AIDS in ways that may be more voyeuristic than medically necessary. Persons who acquire HIV through blood transfusions have been called "innocent victims," suggesting that those with other routes of transmission are guilty and deserve a fatal illness. Internalized homophobia, societal ambivalence about sexuality, and hatred of drug use become interwoven with feelings about the illness. Families often need support for dealing with these unacknowledged, complicated feelings.

Family members without illness, particularly lovers of PWAs, often experience guilt about being healthy. Other family members have fears about their own health status, and fear transmission through contact with the patient. We find it valuable for therapists to initiate discussions of those feelings—to help families realize that their feelings are expectable responses and shared by many experiencing this crisis. Frank discussion of safer sex and transmission of HIV should occur throughout therapy (Hepworth & Shernoff, 1989), and therapists should stay informed about research documenting the lack of HIV transmission to nonsexual household contacts and family members (Fischl et al., 1987; Friedland et al., 1986; Rogers et al, 1990).

Working to limit blame enables families to express anger about the illness, but not let the illness or accompanying resentment take over their relationships and lives. By acknowledging the effect of illness, families can work to "put illness in its place" (Gonzalez, Steinglass, & Reiss, 1989), care for the ill person, and engage in other family activities. This changes a family's focus from *dying from AIDS* to *living with AIDS*.

Maintain Communication

Encouraging family communication is a basic tenet of therapy, but this is a family task often lost during illness crises. Each family member has a unique explanatory model (Kleinman, 1988) that includes their understanding of the illness, the expected consequences, and appropriate treatment and family response. Individual beliefs often are not shared with one another. Families also have shared explanatory models reflecting their historical family patterns of focusing on illness, ignoring it, or communicating directly about the illness.

Families can be encouraged to share their concerns and ideas with one another, perhaps by constructing an illness-oriented genogram, in which family illness history and responses are traced. Such discussion allows family members to recognize their accustomed ways of responding to illness, and to consider how they might prefer to respond. This communication often limits misunderstandings and increases intimacy and the chance for consensual, creative decisions. Early in her illness, Valerie Miro was frightened to discuss her illness, hoping that if she ignored it the illness would go away and her husband would not. Yet she remained angry, distrustful, and unwilling to care for her health. With open communication, Valerie was able to confront her fears and get support from her family to construct a less stressful and more healthy life.

In medical family therapy, communication among therapists, medical providers, and family members is crucial. Family therapists and physicians can be natural partners in health care, and an open, ongoing collaborative relationship is a useful and important goal. Even when therapists and physicians do not work together regularly, they can compare their goals, progress, and unique perspectives about the family. Telephone calls, sharing of written reports, and occasional joint sessions limit the tendency for triangulation. Most important, providers who support one another are able to provide more support to families, and thus help them achieve their desired goals.

When Valerie Miro eventually allowed her providers to talk with one another, Valerie called the physician from the therapist's office and introduced them by telephone. (This could have been usefully done with a speaker phone.) This provided a clear statement that patient and both providers were all involved with care. The providers learned that they had been encouraging Valerie in similar ways. The physician had been asking Valerie to enter therapy for a long time, and the therapist had been asking Valerie to care for herself medically. With phone contact, the providers shared their concerns and treatment plans. Progress notes were exchanged, and the therapist learned more details about Valerie's deteriorating health and helped Valerie discuss her medical status more honestly in therapy. During the last year, the providers exchanged occasional phone calls and met when Valerie was briefly hospitalized.

Reinforce Family Identity

Families with ill members often feel that they are defined more by the illness than by other family goals and identity markers. Medical family therapists prefer the language of *person with AIDS* or *family coping with AIDS*, rather than *AIDS patient* because the former reinforces that there is (first) a person who (second) has an illness. Families may be coping with illness, but they are also families in which children are growing and family members are musical, studious, or eccentric. These special family qualities often are neglected as the illness takes center stage.

Medical family therapists can help families redefine themselves by focusing on how they thought of themselves prior to the illness, or how they would prefer to define themselves now. Families may have difficulty with this task, and state that they cannot do what they want because of the illness. This is the time for creativity, humor, and collective brainstorming. After much consideration, Ava Miro and her family decided they wanted to go camping. They planned an itinerary, rented supplies, read books, and also selected a camp site near a good hospital. They did not require use of the hospital, and enjoyed their 5-day adventure so much that they planned a second trip. The family plans did not exclude the patient or her illness, but did make other family activities and goals a priority.

Enhance Communion

Communion is reflected in the emotional connections within families and between families and outside supports. Medical family therapy encourages families to actively decrease isolation and find support and connection. Therapy, of course, is one form of communion, but should not be a substitute for increasing connections among patients, families, and outside supports.

Some families find it difficult to accept AIDS in a family member, and there are far too many popular stories of patients who were abandoned by families that believed that lesbian and gay male sexual orientation, drug use, or AIDS was morally repugnant. Yet even with such families, opportunities for discussion have sometimes allowed some resolution within the family. Sometimes without the patient present, members can express their upset and disapproval, eventually separate the illness from the person, and allow connections among themselves and the patient. Perhaps as the frequency of AIDS increases, families will continue to hear of other families that experience similar concerns, and family abandonment will be less frequent.

As families focus on illness, and particularly illnesses like AIDS that encourage secrecy, outside social contacts and supports are diminished. For example, Ava Miro's increased responsibility for her grandchildren and sick daughter led Ava to quit her job, miss many of her son's football games, and avoid community gatherings. Once social activities become limited, it can be difficult to begin them again. When friends feel that there is no longer time for them, they may stop calling, and families experience even greater isolation.

Thus, communion with others outside of the family is also important. Connections can be found by rekindling lapsed relationships—perhaps using therapy sessions to brainstorm about who and how to contact. Support groups can be useful in decreasing isolation and encouraging alternative coping styles. Although Valerie Miro refused to attend a support group, her mother participated in a caregiver's support group and gained so much support that she returned to some of her previous activities and began giving talks about her experiences at a local community center.

Increase Agency

Medical family therapists can help patients and families determine what form of medical care they want and how to communicate their desires to medical providers. Many families have little experience negotiating this care, and often feel intimidated by the medical system. Physicians may not initiate discussions about important medical care decisions, but most believe that families should play a part in decision making (Bedell & Delbanco, 1984). Families coping with illness can make their choices explicit, and therefore be more satisfied with their treatment during this stressful period.

Medical family therapists can help families decide what they can handle. In addition to decisions about medical treatment, families often make decisions about how best to provide care. When a patient becomes incapacitated, families may choose to provide full medical care at home, have friends and aides assist, or use an in-home or institutional hospice. Each option results in different family stresses: the burden of travel and guilt if they are not always with the patient, or the inability to obtain respite relief from continuous care.

It can be difficult to learn how to become actively involved in management of an illness. Patients and family members must squarely face the illness and its treatment, and must honestly consider their values and priorities. One family might realize that AIDS dementia in the patient makes it too difficult to care for him or her at home. Medical family therapists can be instrumental in facilitating these significant decisions and providing support after decisions are made. When a family reaches decisions through negotiation and honest sharing, their sense of agency is increased. Perhaps with AIDS, where there seems so little control, it is possible for families to recognize new strengths and abilities.

Face the Inevitability of Death

There are "acceptable" times in the life cycle when death is supposed to occur. AIDS often occurs in young, previously healthy people, unexpectedly affecting their families during active periods of life. Families usually share our general cultural reluctance to consider death (cf. McDaniel et al., 1992). AIDS breaks down a family's denial of death, a gradual process that occurs throughout the course of the illness. Acknowledging the closeness of death frees some families to honestly share their feelings, fears, and plans.

With AIDS, young people lose lovers, children lose parents, and parents outlive children (Walker, 1991). The death of young people and children represents a loss of a family's hopes and dreams. Therapists can help families discuss their intense feelings about these anticipated losses, assisting them to consider one another as resources, rather than as persons on whom to project their anger.

Medical family therapy requires therapists to attend to issues of loss, death, mourning, and grief (Walsh & McGoldrick, 1991). Illnesses and disabilities confront families and providers with issues of mortality. Medical family therapists use the opportunity to encourage families and providers to come together, face realities, and assist one another.

Deal with Unfinished Emotional Concerns

Acknowledging the inevitability of death allows families to "balance their emotional ledgers" (Boszormenyi-Nagy & Spark, 1973). Even for many AIDS patients, who have extended cutoffs from family, there is an urgency to reconnect with family (Landau-Stanton & Clements, 1992; Walker, 1991). This is not the time for family members to share all of their past resentments with one another, but a time to consider what is important to say and what is important to let go.

When Valerie Miro knew that she would die from AIDS, she talked with the medical family therapist about some of the past conflicts she had with her mother. She decided that, although she was angry with her mother for past perceived favoritism toward a sister, she did not need to tell her mother how hurt she had been by the slights. Discussing what she wanted to leave with her mother allowed Valerie to tell her mother that it had not always been perfect, but that she knew she had always been loved. Valerie was pleased that she had expressed her concerns to her mother in ways that helped them feel more forgiveness and closer to one another.

During bereavement, families tend to repeat family patterns regarding loss (Byng-Hall, 1991), and may inadvertently lose the opportunity to be truly intimate. Byng-Hall suggested that the intensity of emotions generated can help families elect corrective scripts and change previous painful patterns. Expressing hopes and identifying treasured memories allow families to change the family legacy about loss (Bowen, 1991). The dying person has the singular opportunity to pass on hopes for the future, and ways in which he or she would like to be remembered.

Help Families Say Good-Bye

Agency is enhanced when families incorporate their own rituals about saying good-bye and grieving. Many families are not aware that they have special practices, and the process of choosing responses helps them find meaning and comfort. Selected rituals should honor the past, alter the present, and enable the future (Imber-Black, 1991). Therapists can help families consider what is meaningful for them.

Identifying helpful practices should be a process of co-creation for the family, with minimal therapist imposition. With the Miros, Valerie's grandmother moved to Puerto Rico, and the family had a good-bye dinner for her. Most believed that this would be the last time the entire family would be together before Valerie's death. Ava and Valerie planned the dinner as a joyous time, where they celebrated their presence together. Valerie stated that she knew she would not see her grandmother again, but she had said good-bye to her privately and did not want that to be the dinner's focus. The Miros used humor, companionship, and prayer to acknowledge their time together and the times they would be apart.

By caring for the ill person and one another, removing disrupting emotional barriers, and creating meaningful rituals, families have the opportunity to say good-bye. Perhaps the long-term legacy of this process is one of the most beneficial outcomes of medical family therapy.

Maintain Empathetic Presence

When illness becomes terminal, patients and families are encouraged to accept what cannot be changed. Therapists, too, must accept that they cannot change outcomes, and realize that empathetic presence, rather than change, may become the goal of therapy. Around the time of death, therapists should be flexible and willing to meet families in the home or the hospital, be available for telephone support, and allow the family to decide about future meetings. Many families appreciate when therapists attend the funeral, and therapists often appreciate the time to say good-bye to the patient.

Families that are actively involved with a medical family therapist during the illness will generally choose to meet, even briefly, following the death. Sessions can help family members feel positive about the choices they made, the ways they cared, and the ways they supported one another. Sometimes with AIDS, bereaved family members may be discouraged that they could not "beat the illness"—that the death represents their failure to care enough. Therapists and physicians can remind families about the biological realities of illness, and help them limit blame toward one another.

Medical family therapists can provide needed support to medical team members around grief and loss. Although the medical family therapist is part of the treatment team, the therapist can be the catalyst for encouraging team members to discuss their responses to this family and this loss, attend funerals, and continue contact as needed with families.

Conclusion

Friends and colleagues often ask how it is possible to work with patients who have a frightening illness like AIDS. Many assume that this therapy is full of sadness, loss, and hopelessness. Certainly the work can be difficult. Therapists treating those who live with AIDS should have professional peer support to discuss their feelings of sadness, loss, and helplessness. Collaboration with medical providers and other medical family therapists also provides necessary support. Most therapists have a balance of patients with different kinds of concerns, not all of which are terminal.

Yet working with people with AIDS has some benefits. When people face a shortened life, they often make decisions about priorities and achieving dreams. They learn that there is not time for wasted activities or relationships. They often make changes in their relationships consistent with their priorities. Working with people who appreciate the present can be deeply meaningful for therapists.

References

Bakan, D. (1969). *The duality of human existence*. Chicago: Rand McNally.

Bedell, S., & Delbanco, T. (1984). Choices about cardiopulmonary resuscitation in the hospital: When do physicians talk with patients? *New England Journal of Medicine, 310*, 1089–1093.

Bloch, D. (1983). Family systems medicine: The field and the journal. *Family Systems Medicine, 1*, 3–11.

Boszormenyi-Nagy, I., & Spark, G. (1973). *Invisible loyalties: Reciprocity in intergenerational family therapy.* New York: Harper & Row.

Bowen, M. (1991). Family reactions to death. In F. Walsh & M. McGoldrick (Eds.), *Living beyond loss: Death in the family* (pp. 79–92). New York: Norton.

Byng-Hall, J. (1991). Family scripts and loss. In F. Walsh & M. McGoldrick (Eds.), *Living beyond loss: Death in the family* (pp. 130–143). New York: Norton.

Centers for Disease Control and Prevention. (1991). Mortality atributable to HIV infection/AIDS–United States, 1981–1990. *JAMA, 265,* 848–849.

Centers for Disease Control and Prevention. (1992, November). HIV/AIDS surveillance report. Washington, DC: U.S. Department of Health and Human Services.

Doherty, W., & Baird, M. (1983). *Family therapy and family medicine: Toward the primary care of families.* New York: Guilford.

Doherty, W. J., Baird, M., & Becker, L. (1987). Family medicine and the biopsychosocial model: The road toward integration. *Marriage and Family Review, 10,* 51–70.

Engel, G.L. (1977). The need for a new medical model: A challenge for biomedicine. *Science, 196,* 129–136.

Fischl, M.A., Dickinson, G.M., Scott, G.B., Klimas, N., Fletcher, M.A., & Parks, W. (1987). Evaluation of heterosexual partners, children, and household contacts of adults with AIDS. *JAMA, 257,* 640–644.

Friedland, G.H., Saltzman, B.R., Rogers, M.F., Kahl, P.A., Lesser, M.I., Mayers, M.M., & Klein, R.S. (1986). Lack of household transmission of HTLV-III infection. *New England Journal of Medicine, 314,* 344–349.

Gonzalez, S., Steinglass, P., & Reiss, D. (1987). *Family-centered interventions for people with chronic disabilities: The eight-session multiple family discussion group program.* Washington, DC: Center for Family Research, George Washington University Medical Center.

Hepworth, J., & Shernoff, M. (1989). Strategies for AIDS education and prevention. In E.D. Macklin (Ed.), *AIDS and families* (pp. 39–80). Binghamton, NY: Haworth.

Imber-Black, E. (1991). Rituals and the healing process. In F. Walsh & M. McGoldrick (Eds.), Living beyond loss: Death in the family (pp. 207–223). New York: Norton.

Kleinman, A. (1988). *The illness narratives.* New York: Basic Books.

Landau-Stanton, J., Clements, C., Cole, R.E., Griepp, A.Z., Tartaglia, A.F., Nudd, J., Espaillat-Pina, E., & Stanton, M.D. (1992). *AIDS, health and mental health: A primary sourcebook.* New York: Brunner/Mazel.

McDaniel, S., Campbell, T., & Seaburn, D. (1990). *Family-oriented primary care: A manual for medical providers.* New York: Springer-Verlag.

McDaniel, S., Hepworth, J., & Doherty, W. (1992). Medical family therapy: A biopsychosocial approach to families with health problems. New York: Basic Books.

Rait, D. (1991). The family context of AIDS. *Psychiatric Medicine, 9*, 423–439.

Ransom, D. (1983). Random notes: On building bridges between family practice and family therapy. *Family Systems Medicine, 1*, 91–96.

Rogers, M.F., White, C.R., Sanders, R., Schable, C., Ksell, T.E., Wasserman, R.L., Bellanti, J.A., Peters, S.M., & Wray, B.B. (1990). Lack of transmission of HIV from infected children to their household contacts. *Pediatrics, 85*, 210–214.

Rolland J. (1984). Toward a psychosocial typology of chronic and life-threatening illness. *Family Systems Medicine, 2*, 245–262.

Rolland, J. (1988). Family systems and chronic illness: A typological model. In F. Walsh & C. Anderson (Eds.), *Chronic disorders and the family* (pp. 30-49). Binghamton, NY: Haworth.

Solomon, G.F., Temoshok, L., & Zich, J. (1987). An intensive psychoimmunologic study of long-surviving persons with AIDS. *Annals of the New York Academy of Sciences, 496*, 647–655.

Walker, G. (1991). *In the midst of winter: Systemic therapy with families, couples, and individuals with AIDS infection.* New York: Norton.

Walsh, F., & McGoldrick, M. (1991). Loss and the family: A systemic perspective. In F. Walsh & M. McGoldrick (Eds.), *Living beyond loss: Death in the family* (pp. 1–29). New York: Norton.

■ ■ ■

4

Language, Silence, and Somatic Fixation

David B. Seaburn, MS

One of the most challenging and rewarding aspects of being a family therapist in an outpatient medical setting is the opportunity to work with patients and families who present a complex picture of physical, emotional, and relational problems. Of particular interest are those patients who are somatically fixated. Somatic fixation occurs when a patient or family focuses entirely on the physical aspects of a complex problem (VanEijk et al., 1983). These patients may vary in the intensity and frequency of physical symptoms. Some patients are always somatically fixated. They focus on a revolving cycle of symptoms that include virtually all bodily systems. Other patients may become somatically fixated only during a health crisis, such as the diagnosis of a new illness or the postoperative period of recuperation. Still others may follow a more episodic course. These patients may have low levels of anxiety about their health almost all the time. Their health anxiety may increase during times of increased emotional stress or physical illness.

Somatically fixated patients do get sick and often have diagnosable conditions. Whether their physical complaints produce clinical findings is not the key factor in defining somatic fixation. The tendency to focus on bodily symptoms and functioning as the primary source of the patient's problems, often to the exclusion of all other factors, is the hallmark of somatic fixation. Emotional, psychological, relational, and spiritual dimensions of the patient's life are often subsumed by worries about the body. Family life may be organized around the individual's physical symptoms. Family members may respond in a multitude of ways, from support, to overinvolvement, to frustration and anger, to helplessness, to withdrawal.

Somatically fixated patients tend to overutilize the health-care system (deGruy, Columbia, & Dickinson, 1987). They have 50% more frequent medical office visits and 50% higher charges. Physicians, mental health providers, and other health-care professionals who treat somatically fixated patients often find themselves somatically fixated in their approach to the patient and family (McDaniel, Campbell, & Seaburn, 1990). This is due to the complicated nature of patients' complaints and the urgency of their requests for help. Consequently, medical providers may overlook other aspects of the patients' life, they may order tests more frequently and inappropriately, and they may feel less competent with such patients and find themselves withdrawing or referring to specialists prematurely or unnecessarily. An analysis of the use of verbal language by somatically fixated patients reveals problems with self-identity, general negativity, and an absence of connection to others (Oxman, Rosenberg, Schnurr, & Tucker, 1985, 1988a, 1988b). This may further contribute to the difficulties that health-care and mental health-care providers often have when working with somatically fixated patients and their families.

Although it is difficult to work with somatically fixated patients, their needs are genuine and profound. Somatically fixated patients often have been physically or sexually abused as children (deGruy et al., 1987; Katon, 1985). They have grown up in families that have experienced significant unresolved losses and trauma (Brodsky, 1984). The interpersonal atmosphere of their families may have been one of chronic, unresolved conflict and a sense of danger or threat. Somatically fixated patients are often unable to communicate their emotional life in any other way than through their symptoms (Brodsky, 1984). They may have learned that the only way to receive support or nurturance is through physical illness. One patient described her father as cold, distant, and physically abusive except when she was ill or hurt, at which point her father was gentle and caring. It is not surprising that the patient was ill during much of her childhood and adolescence. For her, physical symptoms became a means to multiple ends: It protected her from physical abuse, it provided her a way to express her emotional need, and it enabled her to get the love from her father that was usually withheld.

As indicated previously, word choice by somatically fixated patients indicates a distinguishing style of verbal communication. What is most striking and problematic, however, is that there are whole areas of the patient's life for which there seems to be no verbal language. Consequently, the body takes over, articulating what the tongue cannot or is not permitted to articulate. The idea that symptoms may be forms of communication is particularly important when working with somatically fixated patients and their families. Their symptoms are a form of language that needs to be respected for the physical pain it describes and understood for the metaphor of *emotional pain* it also represents. In this chapter, I use concepts derived from social constructionism (Berger & Luckmann, 1966; Bruner, 1986; Efran, Lukens, & Lukens, 1991; Geertz, 1973; Gergen, 1985; Hoffman, 1990; Kelley, 1983; von Glasersfeld, 1987) to discuss the language dilemmas that may contribute to the development of somatic fixation. I also discuss some implications for clinical work. First, I present a case of somatic fixation.

"I Shed No Tears": A Case Example

Luther and Mary are a couple in their early thirties. They have a son, Randy, age 5, and a daughter, Sally, age 3 (see Fig. 4. 1). Luther and Mary lived together for 1 year before getting married 9 years ago. Luther is the oldest of three sons. His father, Harry, lives out of state with Luther's stepmother. Luther's mother died when Luther was 10 years old. She committed suicide. Mary is her parents' only child. Her father, Doug, had three children in his first marriage. His wife died when their youngest child was 1 year old. Mary's father died a year before Luther and Mary got married. Her mother subsequently remarried and also lives out of state. Luther is a successful engineer in a local corporation. Mary works in the home, raising Randy and Sally. The couple describes their marriage as stable and mutually satisfying. Unfortunately, they also agree that things have changed in the last 2 years.

In the spring 2 years ago, Luther developed chronic diarrhea. When the symptoms would not abate, his family physician admitted Luther to a local hospital. He was diagnosed with irritable bowel syndrome. The symptoms were treated with steroids and eventually subsided. But in the spring of the following year, his diarrhea flared up again.

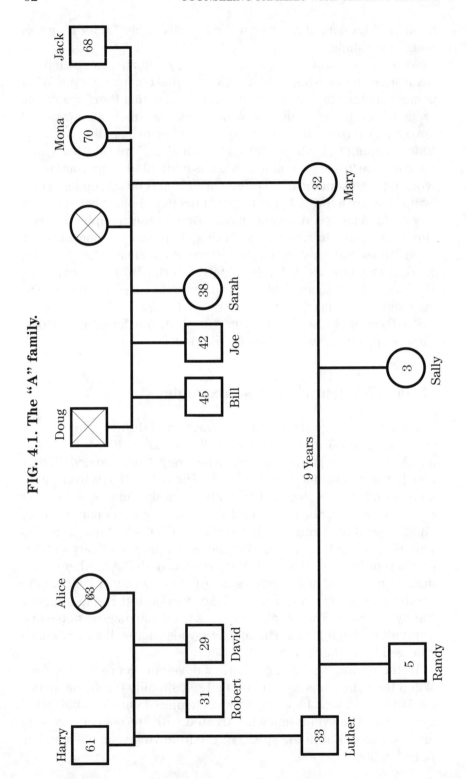

FIG. 4.1. The "A" family.

This time the symptoms were not abating as quickly. Luther became more depressed, and his wife was frustrated with Luther's illness and irritability. Their family doctor recognized the amount of stress they were under and suggested a referral therapy. The couple agreed to the referral, hoping that therapy would help reduce Luther's stress level.

At the initial interview, Luther was anxious and Mary was tearful as they described the events of the previous 2 years. It became apparent that Luther worried chronically about his health and his work. He described being anxious about aches, pains, bumps, and bruises since he was a boy. However, Luther said that this illness was his first bout with "real" health problems.

Luther believed his health problems were due to work-related stress. His job had changed significantly over the last 2 years, including increased responsibilities. He felt more and more was being demanded of him with less time to do it. Seldom was he able to relax, and recently he had been getting angry at the kids more often. Mary agreed and added that the two of them had little time together. Luther's goal for therapy was simple: He wanted to learn how to reduce his stress, and he wanted some exercises or something that would help him relax.

At the end of the first visit, we discussed a few simple strategies for getting started. The couple planned ways to reduce tension at "reentry" time—when Luther came home from work. I encouraged them to go out once as a couple. I also suggested that Luther spend 15 minutes each day as "worry time." He was to list all his worries, prioritize them, and decide which were necessary worries and which were not. Between visits I talked with Luther's doctor about the overall treatment plan. Luther would continue on medication while we worked on stress reduction.

At the next visit, Luther and Mary reported that they had gone out twice. They found it helpful to reconnect. Luther had done his "worry list" and also reported a decrease in the frequency of diarrhea. During his daily "worry time," Luther discovered some things he had not realized: "I was surprised how often I think about my mother. She's been dead so long. I also felt this undercurrent of anger at my father, but I also wish we were closer. He never really talks." Luther's mother had been diagnosed with schizophrenia. She had been hospitalized several times. He remembered that she was often upset and anxious, and that she committed suicide by shooting herself. Because his parents argued a lot, Luther often blamed his father for her death. He talked about his mother's last day:

I remember coming home from school the day she died. There were lots of people outside in the yard, police, and ambulance. Dad told us she was dead, that she killed herself. We went to a neighbor's house until after dinner, then went home. Dad explained that she couldn't take it anymore and bought a gun from the local store and shot herself. I couldn't believe it. We never discussed it again.

During this second visit, Luther also realized that he was now the same age as his mother was when she committed suicide—33. He said he never grieved after she died. Luther had very little to say about his mother or her death. He felt he did not know much about her. His father never talked about her. No one in the family discussed her. I suggested that it might help to learn more about his mother. It is hard to grieve for someone you never knew. For the next visit, Luther kept a journal of recollections about his mother. I also asked him to bring in family pictures. Mary was supportive and agreed to help.

Luther returned with a neatly typed page of memories. He also brought four pictures of his mother and father. The "story" of his mother included these scenes:

- When going to the grocery store, I read the list and got the items because she couldn't handle it.
- She and dad yelled and screamed downstairs after we went to bed.
- She washed my hair over the bathtub and got frustrated by my squirming. She pushed my head under the water and ran away.
- She had uncontrollable shaking of her hands and legs while riding in the car.
- On my 7th birthday, my mother threw a big birthday party for me with all my neighborhood friends over. It was a very happy time for me.
- I remember my first communion. She was very proud of me.
- One time she made a Halloween costume for me—a king's costume with hearts and diamonds and spades and clubs on it.
- She was in and out of the hospital two or three times. I thought she was getting better.
- She protected me against the neighborhood kids who sometimes picked on me. One day she ran out of the house yelling and screaming and chased them all away.
- My brothers and I used to come home for lunch, which she fixed for us. Bacon and beans was a favorite. She fixed this for us on the day that she killed herself.
- I remember shedding no tears at her funeral or after.

These were among the vignettes that formed Luther's memory of his mother; in effect, these stories were Luther's mother. He felt he did not yet know enough about his mother for her to be more than a "one-dimensional" figure to him. He still did not feel any grief. Luther and Mary planned a trip to visit Luther's father and brothers. Luther's father had been calling him more often because of Luther's health problems. Luther planned to learn more about his mother on this trip, but he was hesitant to talk to his father about her. He decided to only talk to his father about his own health, which continued to improve.

At the following visit, 1 month later, Luther and Mary discussed their trip. Luther talked to his brothers about their mother, but they had few memories. Luther then talked to his maternal uncles and learned that his mother had been an excellent high school student. She was valedictorian of her class. Luther learned that his mother's first love, after academics, was ice skating. His uncles described her as ambitious and loving. Luther made a trip to his mother's grave. It was the first in many years, and it was the first time he ever cried over her death. He told his mother that he loved her and that he missed her.

At the next appointment, Luther was feeling much better, emotionally and physically, but was anxious about an upcoming visit from his father. Luther had talked to his father about his irritable bowel problems while on his trip. That went well; his father was genuinely concerned. But Luther had not discussed his mother. Luther and Mary planned a strategy for talking with Luther's father. They decided Luther would take small steps and not expect to accomplish everything at once. The main thing was to begin talking to his father about Luther's mother.

Three weeks later, Luther and Mary reported that the visit with Luther's father had gone very well. Luther talked to his father and, to Luther's surprise, found his father to be very open: "I found out that my mother's folks rejected her over religious issues and over her desire to go to college. In fact, they tried to block her from going. But she was very determined and went anyway."

Luther learned that his mother's emotional problems started after the birth of Luther's next youngest brother. She was later diagnosed with schizophrenia. During that time, her parents "turned their back on her." Luther also learned more about the day she died: "She bought the gun after we went to school. After lunch she went back to the hardware store because she didn't understand how to use it. Then she called dad and left a message for him to come home early. I guess she didn't want one of us kids to find her."

Through the careful reconstruction of his mother's last day, Luther began to understand her desperation. He also recognized how much she loved her children. She cooked them their favorite meal and made sure they would not be the ones to find her when they came home from school. In those ways she protected them, although she could not protect herself.

Luther and Mary also talked at length about his physical illness. His "flare-ups" in the last 2 years had coincided with the anniversary of his mother's last months of life. The most recent flare-up occurred when Luther reached the same age as his mother. They wondered at the coincidence. We discussed the body's "wisdom" and its effort to articulate what had never been said in words.

At the final visit, Luther reported he had received a very helpful letter from his maternal aunt. His father also sent him some home movies of his mother before she became ill. This helped Luther complete a multidimensional view of his mother. Luther also reported that his physical symptoms were gone. He had a recent colonoscopy that indicated he was healing. His doctor was decreasing his medication in accordance with his progress. In many cases, the elimination of physical symptoms is not a reasonable goal. Patients often continue to focus on their body long after therapy is complete. In such cases, the goal is to decrease the influence that anxiety over physical symptoms has in their daily living. These patients, in essence, are helped to be more in charge of their symptoms than their symptoms are in charge of them.

Luther's story fits the profile of many somatically fixated patients. He grew up in an atmosphere of chronic, unresolved parental conflict and some evidence of emotional abuse. He also suffered an early traumatic loss, for which he never grieved. Luther had a history of worry about minor aches and pains. This chronic, low-level anxiety escalated when he developed more problematic symptoms at the same age his mother was when she committed suicide. Essentially, his body brought attention to an area of his life that was unresolved and unrecognized.

Treatment focused on the unspoken dimension of Luther's life and how it blocked his capacity to grieve. What we know of life, we know through "lived experience" (White & Epston, 1990). Our "lived experience" is given meaning through the "storying of experience" (White & Epston, 1990). We "story" our experience through language and dialogue. Through words, actions, and conversation, we develop a shared *Weltanschaung* (Wittgenstein, 1953)—a world view—that is held in common by those with whom we live; a world view that creates order out of our "lived experience" and gives it meaning. With regard to Luther's mother, Luther did not have the opportunity to apply language to his "lived experience"; there was no dialogue over time about this tragedy; he did not have a chance to give his loss a meaning that would help him integrate his mother's death into his life. Luther's mother receded into silence.

The treatment enabled Luther to give some language to his loss. Through therapy, Luther entered into dialogue about his mother. The first dialogue was with himself as he recognized and recorded his own thoughts and feelings—his own inner conversation about his mother and his loss. He then began a "therapeutic conversation" (Anderson & Goolishian, 1988) that included his wife and therapist. Within this small circle of language, Luther began to make sense of his experience, his feelings, and his symptoms. But for that dialogue to have lasting meaning and potential healing, Luther had to converse with his past because it was manifest in the present. He had to go back to move forward (J. Landau-Stanton, personal communication, May 18, 1992). This involved visiting his home of origin, talking to his siblings and relatives, talking with his father, and visiting his mother's grave. Having developed a story of his mother that made her a real person, Luther was able to feel his loss and say good-bye. In the blend of medical treatment and "storying" his experience, Luther's symptoms began to subside. As his emotional wounds started to heal, his physical wounds began to heal as well.

This case is not atypical. Somatically fixated patients who develop language for their emotional and interpersonal lives often experience either the abatement of physical symptoms or a defocusing on physical symptoms that allows them to function more effectively despite ongoing health problems. The interplay of being able to express one's emotional life and experience positive changes in one's physical life is striking. In the next section, I discuss the possible connection between the development of physical symptoms and the loss of language.

Loss of Language and the Emergence of Symptoms

Language, narrative, and story telling has gained much recent attention in a variety of fields, including family therapy (Anderson & Goolishian, 1988; Efran et al., 1991; Hoffman, 1990; White & Epston, 1990), psychology (Bruner, 1986; Geertz, 1973; Gergen, 1985; Sarbin, 1986), medicine (Hunter, 1991; Kleinman, 1988; Seaburn, Lorenz, & Kaplan, 1993; Stein & Apprey, 1990), and philosophy (Quine, 1960;

Rorty, 1979). Much of the work on language in these fields has been influenced by social constructionism (Berger & Luckmann, 1966). Social constructionism is concerned with how people in a particular context describe, explain, and give meaning to the world in which they live (Gergen, 1985). Social constructionism views human beings as reality-creating creatures. Through language and social dialogue, we bring our worlds into existence and give them meaning. *Reality* and *meaning* are not objective in the sense of being contained in the data of everyday life. Instead, we fashion the data of everyday life into a reality through thought and dialogue with others. Once objectified through language, "the reality of everyday life is taken for granted as reality" (Berger & Luckmann, 1966, p. 23).

Luther's case presents the dilemma of the somatically fixated person. What happens when there is no dialogue, no verbal exchange of language, about the data of everyday life? What happens when the data of everyday life includes a mother's suicide? When verbal language is not available to make sense of an experience, what language takes over?

In the following discussion, I present several basic propositions based on social constructionist theory about the role of language in creating a stable, dependable reality. I also speculate on what happens when language and dialogue are not available.

1. *Language plays a central role in establishing the reality and consistency of everyday life.* "I apprehend the reality of everyday life as an ordered reality.... The language used in everyday life continuously provides me with the necessary objectifications and posits the order within which these make sense...to me" (Berger & Luckmann, 1966, pp. 21–22). Through the mundane experience of using words for everything from *mommy* and *daddy* to *peek-a-boo* and *me*, language transforms the world of unknowns into knowable things that have their place in a stable environment. This is reinforced by the fact that when I speak others seem to understand. Through language, I learn that my world is shared; it is intersubjective, and as such is made more stable by this social net of confirmation. My world and those who populate it become firm, dependable, predictable, and unproblematic.

The unproblematic dimension of everyday life is so only until its continuity is upset by a problem. A problem may be understood as an event that does not "fit" into the normal flow of everyday life. A child hears his or her parents arguing downstairs. This may not fit the child's understanding of his or her world. When a problem arises, a common solution is to integrate the problem into what is already unproblematic. The child may disregard what he or she hears; without a way to integrate it, the child may remove it from his or her world and pretend it is not there. Or the child may become upset and seek solace from the parent, who may say "mommy and daddy still love each other." In this way, the child may integrate the problematic into the unproblematic.

In a sense, our knowledge is precarious: "My knowledge of everyday life has the quality of an instrument that cuts a path through a forest and, as it does so, projects a narrow cone of light on what lies just ahead and immediately around; on all sides of the path there continues to be darkness" (Berger & Luckmann, 1966, p. 45). We gain a measure of stability on this path because we share the precariousness of what we know with others.

2. *We are created in relationships with others.* No "organism... or even the self" can be understood "apart from the particular social context in which it is shaped" (Berger & Luckmann, 1966, p. 50). The first and most important context is with parents. They are the pillars of knowledge who pass on to the child what the child accepts as objectively real. If the parents tell the child "You are good" or "You are bad," it is not experienced by the child as an opinion; it is taken by the child as objective fact. The child's world is mediated by parents or parent figures. They are the filters, and the child takes on what is distilled through them. In this way, the transgenerational process passes on an inherited "reality" to the next generation (Boszormenyi-Nagy & Spark, 1973).

This inherited world is not static. Over time, it evolves as the person's world becomes larger and the opportunities for dialogue with others becomes greater. As one's context grows, one's reality is shaped and changed; we revisit what was and alter it to fit what is or what will be. Central to this process is conversation.

3. *Conversation is the most important means of maintaining, modifying, and attributing meaning to the reality of everyday life.* We interact with our world, and in the process we both create and are created by it. The most basic means of interaction with the world is conversation. In everyday life, we are continuously in conversation with those around us and with ourselves. In the process, we maintain, modify, and reconstruct our reality in an ongoing fashion.

Most daily conversation is casual. This is because most daily conversation points to the taken-for-granted nature of our world. A "loss of casualness" (Berger & Luckmann, 1966) signals a break in the normal flow and a potential threat to the taken-for-granted world. Such a break (e.g., the death of a loved one) calls for an increase in dialogue so that participants in the conversation can modify reality enough to integrate its not-taken-for-granted aspects. Without conversation, the "subjective reality of something that is never talked about comes to be shaky" (Berger & Luckmann, 1966, p. 153).

Luther's dilemma, in regard to his mother's death, is that he is bound by the need to create a meaningful reality, but is blocked from the means of doing it—dialogue or conversation. In essence, he has no language for the most important events of his early development. He grew up in a relational context that supported his dilemma through silence.

The death of others, and the threat of our own, are the "problematic" or "not-taken-for-granted" experience par excellence. Some would say the effort to deal with death is the driving force behind all human endeavor (Becker, 1973). The integration of death into one's reality or world view is of paramount importance. Such integration enables an individual to continue to live on after the loss of loved ones and, in some way, anticipate one's own death with a manageable degree of anxiety.

The most effective legitimations of death are those that give the individual a formula for a "correct death" (Berger & Luckmann, 1966, p. 130). One legitimation of death is the creation of individual and family life-cycle models of development (Carter & McGoldrick, 1988; Erikson, 1950; Haley, 1973). For instance, it is common in family therapy to use a life-cycle approach with families to "normalize" their problems and, in effect, reduce the family's anxiety by connecting them with the larger symbolic world of all families. Death is placed at a distance—as the completion of a normative process of development. In this way, individuals can develop a perspective on what constitutes a "correct death."

Luther's mother was a young woman in the so-called prime of her life who killed herself. Her death was out of phase. It was not the completion of a normative process of development. Luther had to make sense of what might be called an "incorrect death." Making sense of death is a tremendous challenge even for those who have family support and a social context in which to converse and grieve. Making sense of death is an almost impossible task for someone who has no words to give death meaning and no conversation through which to learn the language of loss and move on. Without words and conversation, Luther's world was neither solid nor, in a sense, "real." The "subjective reality" of his mother's death became "shaky."

This context of silence is conducive to the development of and focus on physical symptoms. The body expresses what cannot be expressed through words. In the medical setting where I work, we teach family physician residents to always consider the possibility of physical or sexual abuse in patients who are somatically fixated. As with unresolved grief, silence and secrecy are powerful elements in physical and sexual abuse.

Phyllis is a 46-year-old wife and mother of two daughters, ages 12 and 8. Her family initially entered therapy to address the eldest daughter's sporadic compliance with the treatment of her diabetes. As the presenting problem began to resolve, it was apparent that Phyllis, in particular, was not feeling any less stress. She wondered if she had "a problem." She described years of headaches and pain in her jaws. She had been treated for these symptoms, but with no lasting effect. As we shifted our focus to Phyllis's concern, she remembered severe sexual abuse by a neighbor boy that lasted from ages 5 to 8. Phyllis worked hard to articulate her feelings. She also tried to help her husband understand what she was going through. At one point, I suggested that it would be very hard to share her story with her husband, and that perhaps she did not want to at this time. To this Phyllis said, "You don't understand, do you? It's not that I don't want to talk about it, I just don't have any words." It is no wonder that her head ached and her jaws locked. They expressed the pain of having so much to say but no verbal language with which to say it. As with traumatic loss and unresolved grief, silence and secrecy are often power elements in physical and sexual abuse.

Language is the most basic means we have for connecting with our world. It is the primary way we are socialized. Language enables us to name, define, and order our everyday experience. Through language, we learn how to relate to others and find our place in the world. Language is the tool we use to build meaning and to construct reality. A basic problem for somatically fixated patients is that they have lost or never developed the language necessary to articulate their deepest pain. Without words, the body takes over the pain and speaks the unspoken.

Clinical Considerations

The following discussion of clinical considerations is not intended to be exhaustive. More detailed discussion of a biopsychosocial approach to treating somatic fixation has been provided by McDaniel, Hepworth, and Doherty (1992). This discussion is designed primarily to highlight the dimension of language in the treatment of somatic fixation.

1. *Encourage somatically fixated patients to talk about their physical symptoms* (McDaniel et al., 1990). Although this may have the paradoxical effect of decreasing the patient's focus on somatic symptoms, it is not suggested here with that purpose in mind. More important, patients need an opportunity to articulate their experience through whatever means possible. The provider's role in this early process is to create an atmosphere in which patients can tell their stories. The therapist functions as an "ethnographer" (Stein & Apprey, 1990) who is entering a new world that has a foreign language. The patient must teach the therapist about his or her world. For example, a patient was referred to me because of depression related to chronic foot pain. We started the therapy by increasing the focus on the pain so I could learn about her experience and she could share it, perhaps in ways she had not shared before. Together we discovered that "foot pain" was actually six distinct forms of pain that she felt each time she walked. Patients should be encouraged to make lists of their symptoms or keep symptom diaries (McDaniel et al., 1990). The first step is to increase their verbal language and dialogue about their symptoms.

2. *Respect that patients may not have words for their emotional life.* This sounds obvious, but it is often difficult to maintain. Patients whose somatic fixation increases under stress may be demanding and seem manipulative. It is tempting to "cut through" the somatic fixation and get to the "underlying feelings." This surgical approach is usually premature and may reflect the therapist's anxiety more than the patient's need to "open up." Cutting through to the underlying feelings may also encourage a mind–body split that communicates to the patient, "You're not really sick, it's all in your head."

Progress is slow with many somatically fixated patients. Because they do not have words for their emotional life, they may "cooperate" (deShazar, 1982) with us in unusual ways, such as an increased focus on bodily symptoms. This is often an effort to say, "We're going too fast, you're getting too close," "This feels too dangerous," or "You don't understand."

Therapists who work with somatically fixated patients and their families need a high tolerance for the uncertainty and unclarity that are always part of the therapy. A willingness to live with "not knowing" when working with these patients and families is not only a necessity, but a resource (Anderson & Goolishian, 1988). By maintaining a posture of "not knowing," the therapist can remain "curious" about the patient's body language. This helps the therapist resist the urge to change the patient—to make the patient communicate differently before the patient is able.

3. *Listen for the metaphoric communication embedded in the patient's symptom presentation.* One of the most helpful ways to remain curious is to recognize the metaphoric quality of the patient's somatic symptoms. Often the patient's discussion of his or her body provides an excellent map for the terrain of their emotional lives as well. A patient with chronic neck and back pain may talk about "shouldering" a lot of responsibility at work; a patient with "something stuck in my throat" may be keeping a painful secret. One patient who frantically described every part of her body as "out of control" broke into tears, explaining that her daughter had moved out recently. The patient's world, like her body, felt out of control without the steadying presence of her caregiving daughter.

As the therapist becomes attuned to the metaphoric quality of the patient's symptoms, he or she can respond in metaphor as well. I have found that patients are often more willing to talk about other aspects of their lives when I make a metaphoric connection between their symptoms and their broader experience.

A male patient and his wife were seen conjointly by myself and the couple's primary-care physician. The man had been in a serious automobile accident that took the life of the other driver. The patient had suffered mild head trauma. A CT scan showed no permanent damage, despite that the patient complained of constant "dizziness," "neck pain," and "pressure" on his head. We began by making a list of all his symptoms and tracked their progress (or lack of it) over several visits. During this time, the couple was unable to discuss anything else. In one session I finally said, "You've been through so much. You've got all these unexplained symptoms that come and go unexpectedly; your head is always spinning, nothing seems certain. It's almost like your whole life is aching and spinning and full of pressure and uncertainty." Over several visits, using similar comments, the couple began to discuss other aspects of their lives. Of particular importance was the death of the patient's father when the patient was 12.

4. *Introduce new forms of language gradually.* It is helpful to think of somatically fixated patients as *preverbal* regarding certain aspects of their lives. It can be a mistake to assume patients will express feelings in a more direct, verbal manner if they are given enough time to open up. Many patients do not have words to name their feelings. These patients need to learn feeling words before they can engage in feeling talk. With the sexually abused patient who had chronic headaches and jaw pain, I began to create lists of feeling words for her to learn and define for herself (e.g., *anger, fear, loneliness, pain,* etc.). Then we attached those feeling words

to the physical sensations she had. In this way, she began to talk about feelings more. Until then, when she experienced the physical sensations of anger or fear, she felt a need to get away for fear that she would "explode." Her jaws needed to be loosened so that what ached in her head could come out through her voice.

5. *Include others in the conversation.* Luther's progress was dependent on including others in the dialogue about his mother and himself. In effect, Luther changed the meaning of his past by conversing with it in the present. If silence can make the subjective reality of certain events "shaky," then dialogue can make one's subjective reality more solid. (It is not insignificant that one of Luther's goals in medical treatment was to have more solid stools.) By talking with his father, brothers, uncles, and aunt, as well as his mother, Luther refashioned the past and made it more intimate and meaningful. This helped him find words enough to both grieve his mother's death and keep his mother's memory.

By including others, the therapist also learns how physical symptoms, illness, and affect are handled in the family. The therapist can learn how the system may support somatic fixation by encouraging it as a form of emotional currency. The somatically fixated patient, such as Luther, needs the family's permission to change. Change without the support of family is not only difficult, but may be seen as disloyal. The foot-pain patient mentioned earlier grew up in a family in which there were many physical problems, but no permission to acknowledge pain—physical or emotional. The patient struggled with the dilemma of needing help, but feeling "that's not the way we do it." Only after the patient visited her mother, and her mother recognized and acknowledged her daughter's pain, could the patient begin the gradual process of adjusting to her chronic pain.

Conclusion

Anderson and Goolishian (1988) described therapy as a "linguistic event" in which the therapist functions as a "master conversational artist" or "an architect of dialogue." Nowhere is this more true than in working with somatically fixated patients and their families. In large part, the problems of these patients exist in the realm of the "not yet said" (Anderson & Goolishian, 1988). The therapist's task is to enter the "not yet said" through the enigmatic language of the patient's body. The therapist tries not to get lost in the patient's physical language. In the end, the therapist wants to help the patient and family return to the world of that which can be "said."

References

Anderson, H., & Goolishian, H. (1988). Human systems as linguistic systems: Preliminary and evolving ideas about the implications for clinical theory. *Family Process, 27*, 371–393.

Becker, E. (1973). *The denial of death.* New York: Macmillan.

Berger, P., & Luckmann, T. (1966). *The social construction of reality.* Garden City, NY: Doubleday.

Boszormenyi-Nagy, I., & Spark, G.M. (1973). *Invisible loyalties: Reciprocity in intergenerational family therapy.* New York: Harper & Row.

Brodsky, C. (1984). Sociocultural and interactional influences on somatization. *Psychosomatics, 25*, 673–680.

Bruner, J. (1986). *Actual minds, possible worlds.* Cambridge, MA: Harvard University Press.

Carter, B., & McGoldrick, M. (1988). *The changing family life cycle: A framework for family therapy* (2nd ed.). New York: Gardner.

deGruy, F., Columbia, L., & Dickinson, P. (1987). Somatization disorder in family practice. *Journal of Family Practice, 25*, 45–51.

deShazar, S. (1982). *Patterns of brief family therapy: An ecosystemic approach.* New York: Guilford.

Efran, J.S., Lukens, M.D., & Lukens, R.J. (1991). *Language, structure, and change: Frameworks of meaning in psychotherapy.* New York: Norton.

Erikson, E. (1950). *Childhood and society.* New York: Norton.

Geertz, C. (1973). *The interpretation of cultures.* New York: Basic Books.

Gergen, K. (1985). The social constructionist movement in modern psychology. *American Psychologist, 40*, 266–275.

Haley, J. (1973). *Uncommon therapy: The psychiatric techniques of Milton H. Erickson, M.D.* New York: Norton.

Hoffman, L. (1990). Constructing realities: An art of lenses. *Family Process, 29*, 1–12.

Hunter, K.M. (1991). *Doctors' stories: The narrative structure of medical knowledge.* Princeton, NJ: Princeton University Press.

Katon, W. (1985). Somatization in primary care. *Journal of Family Practice, 21*, 257–258.

Kelley, G.A. (1983). *A theory of personality.* New York: Norton.

Kleinman, A. (1988). *The illness narratives: Suffering, healing and the human condition.* New York: Basic Books.

McDaniel, S., Campbell, T., & Seaburn, D. (1990). Integrating the mind-body split: A biopsychosocial approach to somatic fixation. *In Family-oriented primary care: A manual for medical providers* (pp. 248–262). New York: Springer-Verlag.

McDaniel, S.H., Hepworth J., & Doherty, B. (1992). Somatizing patients and their families. In *Medical family therapy: A biopsychosocial approach to families with health problems*. New York: Basic Books.

Oxman, T.E., Rosenberg, S.D., Schnurr, P.P., & Tucker, G.J. (1985). Linguistic dimensions of affect and thought in somatization disorder. *American Journal of Psychiatry, 142*, 1150–1155.

Oxman, T.E., Rosenberg, S.D., Schnurr, P.P., & Tucker, G.J. (1988a). Diagnostic classification through content analysis of patients' speech. *American Journal of Psychiatry, 145*, 464–468.

Oxman, T.E., Rosenberg, S.D., Schnurr, P.P., & Tucker, G.J. (1988b). Somatization, paranoia, and language. *Journal of Communication Disorders, 21*, 33–50.

Sarbin, T.R. (Ed.). (1986). *Narrative psychology: The storied nature of human conduct*. New York: Praeger.

Seaburn, D.S., Lorenz, A., & Kaplan, D. (1993). The transgenerational development of chronic illness meanings. *Family Systems Medicine, 10*(14), 385–394.

Stein, H.F., & Apprey, M. (1990). *Clinical stories and their translations*. Charlottesville, VA: University of Virginia Press.

VanEijk, J., Grol, R., Huygen, F., Mesker, P., Mesker-Niesten, J., vanMierlo, G., Mokkink, H., & Smits, A. (1983). The family doctor and the prevention of somatic fixation. *Family Systems Medicine, 1*, 5–15.

von Glasersfeld, E. (1987). *The construction of knowledge*. Salinas, CA: Intersystems Publications.

White, M., & Epston, D. (1990). *Narrative means to therapeutic ends*. New York: Norton.

Wittgestein, L. (1953). *Philosophical investigations*. New York: Oxford University Press.

■ ■ ■

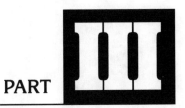

PART

ETHICAL AND PSYCHOSPIRITUAL ISSUES IN TREATMENT

5

Ethical Issues in the Treatment of Families with Chronically Ill Members

Michael C. Gottlieb, PhD

Traditionally, psychotherapy was conducted on an individual basis, and ethical principles were written accordingly (Woody, 1990). The principles were relatively clear, and the lines of professional responsibility generally unambiguous. A psychologist's primary obligation was to his or her client, whose autonomy and welfare he or she was to promote (American Psychological Association, 1990).

Marital and family therapy has been practiced since the early 1950s (Hoffman, 1981), and has received much empirical support. Yet, perhaps due to its more complex nature, few scholarly articles have appeared regarding the ethical issues related to this practice (e.g., Boszormenyi-Nagy & Krasner, 1980; Grosser & Paul, 1964; Hines & Hare-Mustin, 1978; Karpel, 1980; Rinella & Goldstein, 1980).

It was not until 1982 that the ethical issues in family therapy were defined and organized in two seminal works (Margolin, 1982; O'Shea & Jessee, 1982). Since then, some articles have updated this work (e.g., Margolin, 1986; Patten, Barnett, & Houlihan, 1991), added basic issues (Gottlieb, in press), and applied these concepts to different areas of family therapy practice (e.g., Gottlieb & Cooper, 1990, 1993). In 1992, psychology made its first official effort to address these issues in its revised ethical principles (American Psychological Association, 1992).

The purpose of this chapter is to define and discuss these ethical principles with regard to families with chronically ill members. Five major ethical issues are discussed: (a) definition of the client, (b) confidentiality, (c) informed consent, (d) therapeutic neutrality, and (e) justice.

Two assumptions underlie the discussion. First, the chapter addresses only those families in which a child or adult member suffers from a chronic illness. Acute illnesses present different issues beyond the scope of this work. Second, the chapter is limited to families in which there was no premorbid dysfunction. That is, to better illustrate the ethical issues, the chapter is restricted to healthy families that have found it necessary to reorganize due to the chronic illness. In the first part of the chapter, I give the reader a sense of the complexities of these issues by raising many ethical questions that arise when treating families with chronically ill members. Recommendations for practice are made at the end of the chapter.

Definition of the Client

In the most recent revision of its ethical principles, the American Psychological Association (APA; 1992) stated that, "When a psychologist agrees to provide services to several persons who have a relationship (such as husband and wife or parents and children), the psychologist attempts to clarify at the outset (1) which of the individuals are patients or clients and (2) the relationship the psychologist will have with each person" (p. 1605). Family psychologists typically consider the family system as the focus of treatment, and feel ethically obliged to work for the benefit of all (Margolin, 1982). But when families present with chronically ill members, who is the client?

The Identified Patient

The term *identified patient* (IP; Hoffman, 1981) refers to a symptomatic family member who is presented for treatment by his or her family. A family systems-oriented psychologist assumes that the IP is not "ill," but serves the function of *symptom bearer* for family dysfunction. This metaphor serves as a useful concept for understanding family functioning, but should a family psychologist make assumptions applicable to functional disorders in circumstances where a biologically based disease has been documented? For example, is it appropriate to consider a child with diabetes an IP? Is the family psychologist justified in viewing the family as the focus of treatment and denying care to an individual family member who may require it? Dare the family psychologist ignore the possibility that a diabetic family member's poorly managed condition may be related to a dysfunctional family system?

Resistance

Frequently, a major task of the family psychologist is to redefine the IP's problem as one belonging to all family members, so as to establish the family, rather than the IP, as the client. Family psychologists are trained to anticipate and manage resistance to this interpretation, which is intended to disrupt the homeostatic balance of a dysfunctional family system.

Is it appropriate to assume resistance when treating families with chronically ill members? For example, is it ethically appropriate to assume that a family is resistant to family therapy because it does not accept the diagnosis of an early-onset Alzheimer's Disease in their 45-year-old mother? How should the family psychologist proceed if the diagnosis is clear and, in denying her condition, the family exposes the mother to needless danger?

Theoretical Issues

Maintaining a systemic orientation may create ethical dilemmas. First, conflict may arise between the family psychologist and other professionals responsible for the ill member's care. For example, an attending physician may not be sympathetic to the need for family therapy. Furthermore, if family therapy is offered instead of individual treatment, the physician may be troubled if he or she views the patient as not receiving the individual therapy that he or she feels is indicated. A similar problem may arise if the ill member is hospitalized. The staff may not be supportive of the systemic notion that the family is the focus of treatment, especially if it entails greater responsibility and more work for them (Gottlieb & Cooper, 1993).

A second dilemma arises when reporting treatment information to insurance companies. Because insurance companies use a medical model, they expect to receive a diagnosis on an individual patient. If a family psychologist has chosen to make a relational diagnosis, he or she may not be reimbursed. Alternatively, making an individual diagnosis may confuse the family and/or impede the treatment process (Gottlieb & Cooper, 1993).

Confidentiality

Psychologists are ethically obliged to discuss the relevant limitations of confidentiality and the "foreseeable uses of information generated through their services" (American Psychological Association, 1992, p. 1606). In addition, family psychologists are responsible for determining how confidential information between family members is managed (O'Shea & Jessee, 1982). In considering this decision, four alternatives are available.

No Secrets

The first alternative is to keep no information confidential from other family members. This choice makes treatment less complicated and easier to manage for the therapist, but it risks losing important information that family members may not wish to divulge to others. For example, a woman who withholds knowledge of deterioration in her physical condition to avoid "hurting" her loved ones might have benefited had she shared the information with a supportive therapist.

There are times when this approach may be inappropriate. For example, parents draw generational boundaries with their children by not discussing certain issues with them, such as financial matters and their sexual relationship. A "no secrets" policy also may be contraindicated when treating families with older adolescents if it hinders their efforts at separation/individuation (Gottlieb & Cooper, 1990).

Maintaining Confidentiality

A family psychologist may choose to maintain confidentiality with all family members as if they were individual clients. In this way, more information may be revealed privately. Unfortunately, the family psychologist risks reduced maneuverability, triangulation into family conflict, boundary problems (Haley, 1976), and harm to other family members.

What is the family psychologist to do if given information in confidence by one family member that would have direct impact on the well-being of another? Can the family psychologist maintain confidentiality when a husband reveals that he is HIV positive, but asks that his wife not be informed? How can the information be held in confidence without risking harm to the wife, for whom the family psychologist is equally responsible?

Maintaining Some Confidences

One may adopt an intermediate position, in which some information may be kept confidential. Unfortunately, it is impossible to know in advance which information should be kept confidential and which should be shared. For example, a wife may ask her family psychologist to keep confidential that she once contracted a sexually transmitted disease that affected her ability to have children. She makes her request because the information is embarrassing to her, and she assures the therapist the information is unimportant to her husband, who is not interested in having children. Agreeing to do so accepts the wife's assumption that the information would be of no consequence to the husband, and therefore of no systemic importance. But what if the therapist learns that the wife has lied about his feelings or that he has changed his mind and now wants a child? In this case, keeping such information confidential may compromise the treatment process by colluding with the wife, and may risk harming the husband.

Another possible dilemma involves keeping information confidential with the intention of revealing it at some later point (Hines & Hare-Mustin, 1978). For example, a family psychologist was consulted by a woman who presented with complaints regarding the sexual relationship with her husband. The psychologist recommended a conjoint session to further assess the problem and she agreed, but at the appointed hour the husband arrived without his wife. The psychologist, aware of the potential conflict of interest that could arise if she saw him individually, decided to explain the limits of confidentiality and her responsibility to his wife at the outset of the session. Unfortunately, before she could do so, the husband blurted out that he was gay, had known this before marrying, continued to have frequent high-risk sexual liaisons, and that his wife knew none of this. He acknowledged feeling horrible for deceiving her, but justified his decision based on the assumption that if she were to learn the truth, she would divorce him and try to keep him from their children. He desperately wanted to stay with his family, and asked the psychologist to help him tell his wife the truth and end the deception (Gottlieb, in press).

What is the family psychologist to do? An obvious choice is referral because the knowledge obtained places the psychologist in an untenable conflict of interest. But what if the psychologist accepts the husband's request, believing that it was the only hope the wife has to learn this vital information? Briefly maintaining confidentiality with an agreed deadline and temporarily suffering the conflict of interest might be indicated if it were to eventually benefit the wife. Unfortunately, the family psychologist risks being caught in an appalling dilemma. If the husband reneges, she will have to keep vital information, which directly affects the wife's well-being, from the client, to whom she is primarily responsible (Gottlieb, in press).

Therapist's Choice

A final alternative involves maintaining or revealing confidences based on clinical issues, rather than the requests of individual family members (Wendorf & Wendorf, 1985). For example, information might be shared if it were harmful to others, held systemic value, or had important treatment implications (Gottlieb & Cooper, 1990). This approach provides a therapist great latitude. But even if family members are informed of the policy at the outset, they may still feel betrayed when the information is subsequently revealed.

When Circumstances Change

One's policy regarding confidentiality may have to be revised in accordance with changing circumstances. For example, a family psychologist has treated a girl with sickle cell anemia since she was very young. Upon entering her teenage years, she begins to ask that certain information be kept in confidence from her parents. As a function of her developmental level, is she now entitled to some degree of confidentiality? Should the family psychologist change an existing no secrets policy in response to her request? What if the parents object to the change, claiming that the existing policy is still in their daughter's best interest?

A change in policy also may be needed if an adult with a progressive neurological disorder deteriorates to the point where he or she is no longer competent. At this juncture, information he or she reveals may have to be shared with family members for his or her own protection. However, should the afflicted family member be excluded from decision making that directly affects his or her own welfare?

Informed Consent

Psychologists are required to obtain appropriate informed consent for professional procedures in a way that is reasonably understandable to participants. Although the content may vary depending on the circumstances, informed consent requires that the person has the capacity to consent, has been given significant information regarding contemplated procedures, and has consented freely (American Psychological Association, 1992).When working with the chronically ill, some family members may not be competent to consent. In such cases, psychologists are obliged to obtain permission from a legally authorized person, inform the disabled individual in a manner commensurate with his or her ability to understand, seek the individual's assent, and consider his or her preferences and best interest (American Psychological Association, 1992).

Autonomy Versus Paternalism

Promotion of and respect for the autonomy of others is a basic principle of biomedical ethics (Beauchamp & Childress, 1983) and is codified in most professional ethics codes (e.g., American Psychological Association, 1990). Psychologists are expected to "accord appropriate respect to the fundamental rights of all people. They respect the rights of individuals to ...self-determination and autonomy" (American Psychological Association, 1992, p. 1599). Similarly, family psychologists work to foster the autonomy of all family members (Margolin, 1982), but are aware that individual autonomy may be sacrificed in some dysfunctional family systems (e.g., Haley, 1980).

Paternalism entails acting on behalf of another as a benevolent father. It presumes that the motivation of the decision maker is benevolent, and that an individual's autonomy should be overruled because he or she is not fully capable of making an informed decision (Beauchamp & Childress, 1983).

Although it is our mandate to work for the autonomy of our clients, we do not always know the capacity for autonomy of chronically ill family members. For example, an 18-year-old diabetic teenage boy requests an extended vacation touring Europe with his friends for his high school graduation present. According to his parents, although he is healthy, he has been inconsistent about monitoring and managing his insulin requirements all of his life. As a matter of promoting his autonomy, should he be allowed to make the trip even though doing so may expose him to danger? A paternalistic intervention would certainly keep him safe, but is his safety worth the sacrifice of an age-appropriate desire for autonomy?

How Much Information to Reveal

The new APA Ethical Principles (American Psychological Association, 1992) repeatedly emphasize that information must be communicated in a way that is "reasonably understandable" to clients at a level commensurate with their ability to understand. Treatments for clients who are mentally retarded or who suffer from dementia present examples where the family psychologist may face ethical dilemmas when following these obligations. But more complex problems may arise when one is uncertain about a client's capacity to consent.

For example, a competent adult is informed that he has an incurable carcinoma. He seems unable to absorb much information regarding his condition at first, and exhibits a high level of denial. The attending physician argues that this is an expected reaction, and that his capacity for integrating information will improve over time as he adjusts to his condition. But what if the man continues to deny the gravity of his condition? What is the family psychologist to do if his defenses remain rigid and his level of denial so pervasive that other family members are prevented from discussing his condition with him? Is it appropriate for the family psychologist to restrict him- or herself to information the client can reasonably understand? If so, the family may be harmed by being prevented from dealing with the death of its loved one. However, in the interest of the other family members, does the therapist have the right to override the ill member's defenses and confront him with his condition? Furthermore, what is the likelihood that such an intervention would be effective?

Taking the Client's Preferences Into Account

Another new element in the APA Ethical Principles is that, even when working with incompetent individuals, we seek their assent and take their preferences into account. Such a requirement can create troubling ethical problems. For example, what if a 25-year-old female who has spina bifida with some intellectual deficits expressed a strong desire to move into her own apartment, even though there was reason to believe that she lacked the capability and judgment to do so successfully? If she were allowed to move out and failed, might the experience benefit her? Is the experiment worth exposing her to potential harm? Fostering her autonomy may be a disservice, but paternalistically restricting her and not taking her preference into account might prevent her from achieving a greater degree of autonomy.

Freedom

A basic requirement of informed consent is that the client is free to make decisions without influence or coercion from others (Beauchamp & Childress, 1983). This issue is most easily highlighted when the family has an ill member who is dependent on others for his or her care. For example, a family cares for an elderly father who is incapacitated due to advanced arthritis. In an individual session, the father expresses concern that his son has a serious gambling problem. The family psychologist wishes to raise the issue with the family, but the father objects, fearing that his son will terminate therapy and retaliate by placing him in a nursing home.

Does the family psychologist have the right to override the father's request to help other family members? If the father's wishes are respected, how is further treatment to be effective if the father does not feel free to disclose his concerns?

Therapeutic Neutrality

Kitchener (1984) has argued that fidelity is another basic ethical obligation for psychologists: Fidelity "involves questions of faithfulness, promise keeping, and loyalty" (p. 51), and is important because these issues form the basis of trust. It is easier for the individual therapist to meet this obligation because he or she is free to support the client and see the world from the client's perspective. Family psychologists who work with multiple clients in an inherently more confusing situation (Karasu, 1980) generally contend that it is best to remain neutral, not aligning with any particular member or group (Margolin, 1982). Neutrality may be accomplished in one of three ways (Sider & Clements, 1982): (a) promoting the system, (b) changing allegiances, and (c) maintaining no allegiances.

Promoting the System

One may decide to work for the good of the system rather than any individual. Margolin (1982) has supported this alternative, arguing that, because families often have conflicting goals, the family psychologist is in a unique position to be helpful by treating the family system from a neutral perspective. This approach is appealing in its simplicity and may be beneficial in many situations, but can be of limited value when treating families with chronically ill members because what may be best for some family members may not be in the best interest of all (Hines & Hare-Mustin, 1980; Sider & Clements, 1982).

For example, a family psychologist is asked to treat a family with a chronically ill child. The family is lower middle class, has limited health insurance, both parents work outside the home, and the child requires constant supervision and care. When the parents are not home, the other children are expected to help because the family lives far from family and friends. How is the family psychologist to work for the benefit of all family members when each one must sacrifice to care for the chronically ill member?

Changing Allegiances

A therapist may decide to align with different subsystems at different times, assuming that neutrality will be achieved over the course of treatment. Boszormenyi-Nagy and Krasner (1980) argued that the therapist must be prepared to align with all family members sooner or later, but Hines and Hare-Mustin (1978) cautioned that the therapist must be careful not to have it appear as if alignment with one occurs at the expense of another.

The therapist who chooses this option must make rapid and frequent choices regarding alignment in a constantly changing context. How are such decisions to be made? Sider and Clements (1982) argued that in this approach the therapist must work from a hierarchy of values that forms the basis for the shifts in allegiance. They cautioned that this approach has two disadvantages. First, it may have disruptive long-term effects if the therapist's values are unwittingly communicated to the family. Second, they noted that without "rigorous grounding," the therapist might assume an ethical position consistent with prevailing social attitudes, rather than those of the family.

Maintaining No Allegiances

A third possibility is to maintain no allegiances and position oneself as only working to achieve the family's stated goals. Such a posture may avoid ethical dilemmas when the goal of treatment is objective and the family agrees that it is in everyone's benefit to pursue it.

For example, family members may require a psychoeducational intervention to learn how their loved one may be affected by multiple sclerosis. Unfortunately, clinical situations are seldom so clear-cut; Sider and Clements (1982) argued that therapists are seldom able to function in such a value-free manner.

When Neutrality Must Be Abandoned

There are at least four circumstances under which neutrality must be abandoned. Margolin (1982) originally noted three. The first occurs when a family member is trying to leave a relationship, such as a wife who wishes a divorce or an adolescent who wishes to separate from his or her family. The second arises when one family member's goal may be to change the behavior of another, but the other believes that the goal is mutual change. In both cases, neutrality cannot be sustained when the parties have competing goals. The third exception occurs when legal requirements regarding the welfare of an individual take precedence over neutrality, such as mandatory reporting of child abuse.

Many family psychologists work from a developmental perspective, similar to that of family physicians, and treat families over the course of the life cycle. Although a desirable approach, this orientation to practice may create a fourth exception if it becomes necessary for the therapist to advocate for the welfare of one family member over that of another. This dilemma arises in cases such as: (a) encouraging caregiver vacations, (b) helping parents understand the effect of a chronically ill child on their adolescent siblings, or (c) facing the need to institutionalize a loved one.

Justice

Justice means that equal persons have the right to be treated equally and that nonequal persons have the right to be treated differently if the inequality is relevant (Beauchamp & Childress, 1983; Kitchener, 1984). Rawls has argued that justice is best explicated in terms of fairness—that is, that resources should be distributed equally unless an unequal distribution would work to everyone's advantage (Beauchamp & Childress, 1983).

Some of the most vexing ethical questions surround how resources can be fairly allocated when a family has a chronically ill member. In recent years, the United States has experienced a shrinking economy, reduced government spending for health care and social services, the birth of managed care, and the loss of insurance benefits due to unemployment. Virtually everyone has been touched by these trends, but those families with chronically ill members are disproportionately affected because they are increasingly forced to use personal resources to help their disabled loved ones.

For example, should a family expend precious financial resources on an experimental, but nonreimbursable, treatment for an ill child? If it were a matter of spending limited savings, one might argue that the risk was worth the potential benefit, but what if those savings were allocated for another sibling's college education? Is it fair to spend the savings to benefit one child at the expense of another? Conversely, at what point should resources be diverted from the chronically ill family member to assist others in need? For example, should funds be diverted to provide respite to a caregiver? In these situations, how are needs to be assessed and everyone treated fairly?

Guidelines

In considering the following guidelines, some limitations should be noted. First, at times I have made arbitrary distinctions to illustrate ethical issues, which may not correspond to the reality of clinical practice. Second, although I have confined myself to a discussion of ethical issues, the experienced practitioner will note that sound ethical decision making is often indistinguishable from good treatment decisions. Third, the difficulty of managing complex families precludes a list of definitive recommendations; however, the following guidelines may be of assistance.

1. It is generally advisable to consider the family system as the client and to avoid the metaphor of the *identified patient* because it is more appropriately applied to those with functional disorders (McDaniel, Hepworth, & Doherty, 1992). One way or another, the family psychologist must clarify the nature of the professional relationship with each family member from the outset (American Psychological Association, 1992).
2. Resistance may be encountered soon after diagnosis when the client and/or family has not yet accepted the chronicity or severity of the condition, or that everything that can be done has been done. In such cases, resisting a drastic diagnosis of a loved one and seeking all possible avenues of assistance are not pathological behaviors, but part of the normal process of adjustment. At such times, initiating family therapy at this point may be pre-

mature. Instead, it may be best to provide support until the family adjusts to and accepts its new condition. If the family chooses to pursue treatment shortly after diagnosis, the therapist's first job may have to be helping the family accept that which it abhors.

3. Family psychologists will encounter numerous other professionals who may not be sympathetic to a systems perspective when working with chronically ill populations. Despite theoretical differences, it is the family psychologist's obligation to collaborate and treat other professionals with respect as a matter of promoting the family's welfare.

4. Working from a systemic perspective may create problems with insurance reimbursement. Nevertheless, all forms must be completed accurately. To do otherwise may constitute fraud.

5. Many alternatives exist regarding the management of confidential information, and choices may vary with the clinical situation. Nevertheless, it is the family psychologist's obligation to inform the family at the outset of treatment regarding his or her policy in this regard (American Psychological Association, 1992; Hines & Hare-Mustin, 1978; Margolin, 1982). Whenever possible, the policy should consider the possible long-term nature of the professional relationship, and take into account those changes that are likely to occur over the family life cycle.

6. Psychologists work to enhance the autonomy of their clients (American Psychological Association, 1992). In cases where one's autonomy may be compromised, careful assessment is of critical importance. When a family member's competence is unclear, decisions to paternalistically intervene should be made on a conservative basis, giving ill family members every opportunity to attain or maintain their maximum level of autonomy. Paternalistic intervention without consent should be considered only in the face of immanent danger.

7. Treating family members whose competence has been compromised requires an appreciation for and understanding of their level of functioning. Every effort should be made to communicate with them in ways they will understand, taking their preferences into account (American Psychological Association, 1992).

8. As with confidentiality, the family psychologist should have a policy regarding the issue of therapeutic neutrality, and he or she should explain it to the family at the outset of treatment. Although the family psychologist should try to remain evenhanded or balanced in his or her approach, at times it may be necessary to intervene on behalf of one family member. When such inter-

ventions cannot be avoided, they must be made with great care and sensitivity. If neutrality must be compromised, every effort should be made to reestablish it over the subsequent course of treatment.

9. Working with this population often requires dealing with family values. When those values differ from those of the family psychologist, it is his or her obligation to be aware of such differences when they arise, treat the values of the family with respect, and guard against imposing his or her own values on the family.

10. It is necessary for the family psychologist to work with these families from a developmental perspective. The family's circumstances will change as it progresses through the life cycle, necessitating attention to different issues or family members at different times. Family psychologists must be highly flexible, accepting that changes in format (Gottlieb, in press; Margolin, 1982) may occur at numerous points in the family's development.

11. Long periods of time may elapse without contact with the family. Nevertheless, it is prudent to assume that the possibility of renewed treatment never ends, and that the family may wish to resume the professional relationship at any point in the family life cycle.

12. Ultimately, families will make their own decisions regarding the allocation of resources, but they may look to the family psychologist for guidance. In such cases, the family psychologist should play the role of an ethics educator, explaining the various alternatives along with their advantages and disadvantages, and helping the family explore these from both aspirational and practical viewpoints. To do so effectively, the family psychologist must be well grounded with relevant empirical data, have formal training in ethics, and have a clear understanding of his or her own values.

Conclusion

The goal of this chapter was to define and discuss various ethical issues that arise in working with families with chronically ill members, and to offer guidelines for practice with this population. As noted, working with this population of families is complex and difficult, and practitioners inexperienced in the area may choose to avoid it. Nevertheless, well-trained systems-oriented family psychologists have a unique and valuable role to play as part of the treatment team. First, they are trained to appreciate and treat a wide range of problems that the family must confront, rather than serving in a restricted or specialized role, as do most other treatment team members. Second, family psychologists working from a developmental perspective and trained in brief therapy techniques can be especially helpful during times of limited financial resources. Finally, family psychologists understand that the treatment team is a system as well; using their consultation and collaborative skills, they are in a position to help the team function at its maximum level of effectiveness.

References

American Psychological Association. (1990). Ethical Principles of psychologists. *The American Psychologist, 45*, 390–395.

American Psychological Association. (1992). Ethical Principles of psychologists and Code of Conduct. *American Psychologist, 47*, 1597–1611.

Beauchamp, T., & Childress, J. (1983). *Principles of biomedical ethics.* New York: Oxford University Press.

Boszormenyi-Nagy, I., & Krasner, B. (1980). Trust-based therapy: A contextual approach. *American Journal of Psychiatry, 137*, 767–775.

Gottlieb, M.C. (in press). Ethical dilemmas for family psychologists and systems therapists: Change of format and live supervision.

Gottlieb, M.C., & Cooper, C.C. (1990). Treating individuals and families together: Some ethical considerations. *The Family Psychologist, 6*, 10–11.

Gottlieb, M.C., & Cooper, C.C. (1993). Some ethical issues for family psychologists practicing in hospital settings. *Family Relations, 42*, 140–144.

Grosser, G., & Paul, N. (1964). Ethical issues in family group therapy. *American Journal of Orthopsychiatry, 34*, 875–884.

Haley, J. (1976). *Problem solving therapy: New strategies for effective family therapy.* San Francisco: Jossey-Bass.

Hines, P., & Hare-Mustin, R. (1978). Ethical concerns in family therapy. *Professional Psychology: Research and Practice, 9*, 165–171.

Hoffman, L. (1981). *Foundations of family therapy.* New York: Basic Books.

Karasu, T.B. (1980). The ethics of psychotherapy. *American Journal of Psychiatry, 137*, 1502–1512.

Karpel, M. (1980). Family secrets: I. Conceptual and ethical issues in the relational context: II. Ethical and practical considerations in therapeutic management. *Family Process, 19*, 295–306.

Kitchener, K.S. (1984). Intuition, critical evaluation and ethical principles: The foundation for ethical decisions in counseling psychology. *The Counseling Psychologist, 12*, 43–55.

Margolin, G. (1982). Ethical and legal considerations in marital and family therapy. *American Psychologist, 37,* 788–801.

Margolin, G. (1986). Ethical issues in marital therapy. In N. Jacobson & A. Gurman (Eds.), *Clinical handbook of marital therapy* (pp. 621–638). New York: Guilford.

McDaniel, S.H., Hepworth, J., & Doherty, W.J. (1992). *Medical family therapy: A biopsychosocial approach to families with health problems.* New York: Basic Books.

O'Shea, M., & Jessee, E. (1982). Ethical, value and professional conflicts in systems therapy. In J.C. Hansen (Ed.), *Values, ethics, legalities and the family therapist* (pp. 1–22). Rockville, MD: Aspen.

Patten, C., Barnett, T., & Houlihan, D. (1991). Ethics in marital and family therapy: A review of the literature. *Professional Psychology: Research and Practice, 22,* 171–175.

Rinella, V., & Goldstein, M. (1980). Family therapy with substance abusers: Legal considerations regarding confidentiality. *Journal of Marital and Family Therapy, 6,* 319–326.

Sider, R.C., & Clements, C. (1982). Family or individual therapy: The ethics of modality choice. *American Journal of Psychiatry, 139,* 1455–1459.

Wendorf, D., & Wendorf, R. (1985). A systemic view of family therapy ethics. *Family Process, 24,* 443–460.

Woody, J.D. (1990). Resolving ethical concerns in clinical practice: Toward a pragmatic model. *Journal of Marital and Family Therapy, 16, 133–150.*

■ ■ ■

6

Personal Ease, Physical Disease, and Intergenerational Family Experience

Donald S. Williamson, PhD

T his chapter expresses the author's reflections on how individuals make decisions about physical health, and on how relationships with personal physicians can promote well-being. Personal well-being, to whatever degree present, emerges in all the important dimensions of human experience—namely, the physical, the psychospiritual, and the social. This chapter focuses particularly on the psychospiritual context for physical well-being, and how this relates to the larger social context. There is special reference to the individual's family-of-origin experiences, as they model and teach about health.

Four interrelated propositions are presented, and are believed to be of compelling importance for the understanding, achievement, and maintenance of physical well-being. These four assumptions find quite different places on the continuum from speculative to databased propositions. However, all grow out of professional experiences of the author, who has worked for over 30 years in both psychological and medical education/treatment settings, as well as with a variety of religious communities. The author has spent the last 6 years, prior to the fall of 1992, working as a family psychologist on the faculty of a department of family medicine. Much of this chapter's thinking grows out of that experience.

Proposition One: Decisions That Influence Physical Health Are Made First At the Level of Mind and Spirit, and the Consequences Are Then Expressed in the Body As Sensations and Symptoms

The first proposition is that, for most people most of the time, physical disease begins with a loss of psychological ease. Therefore, it is inferred that disease frequently expresses "decisions" made at the psychospiritual level. This does not deny the regular occurrence of genetic anomalies or diminish the significance of heredity. Nor does it deny the widespread prevalence of individual biological predispositions and vulnerabilities to physical disease in general, and to specific physical diseases in particular.

Further, it does not ignore that physical disease can escalate to the point where it dominates an individual's experience and controls his or her behavior to the point where the disease appears to be functioning autonomous. Hence, at some point, the disease may be responsive only to biomedical intervention, and eventually not even to that. Nonetheless, "decisions" about personal physical health are not made exclusively by or within the body, although the implications or consequences are revealed in the body. Rather, these decisions are made within the individual's mind and spirit.

(It should be noted, tangentially at this point, that the term *spirit* does not refer to any particular religious dogma, tradition, or practice. It simply refers to that dimension of consciousness where there is either more freedom or else more constriction of the self, more good hope or more fear, more goodwill or more hatred, more open-mindedness or more arrogance, more energy or more lethargy of spirit. This author believes that this psychospiritual expression of human experience and consciousness cannot be reduced to, and is not usefully identified and communicated through, the language of purely psychological categories.)

It may be that the use of the term *decision* here, as in the phrase "healthy decisions," is misleading because it seems to imply that these sequences are conscious, voluntary, willful, and therefore blameworthy. It is far from it. Suicidal behavior, on a continuum, ranges from a self-destructive act that is demonstrably by the individual's own hand, to more subtle and obscure patterns of behavior, which on closer observation simply do not appear to serve well the individual's own success and well-being. Despite this fact about self-destructive behavior, clearly it is a rare individual who actively chooses not to be well. But many health decisions are made at levels of consciousness, or rather *unconsciousness*, that are, by definition, not in awareness. Furthermore, many decisions are made by default (i.e., simply by not taking positive health-promoting or illness-preventing action).

In taking personal responsibility for these decisions, the individual does not need to feel a concomitant guilt or to develop a sense of having been a failure because of this illness. Instead, there is an opportunity here to develop more profound compassion for the foibles of humanness, and the humanness of the self. Not to take responsibility for one's own experiences in life, including illness experiences, increases the sense of personal helplessness in a capricious world. It also encourages undue dependency on the judgment and skill of others (Cousins, 1989). Both of these attitudes lead to a loss of self. This becomes a further threat to personal well-being.

The Alcoholics Anonymous (AA) movement learned early on (as substance-abuse treatment learned later) that there may be rich psychological explanation for an alcoholic's or an addict's behavior, even to the point where the behavior could have been predicted has highly likely. However, it is only as the individual claims ownership of and responsibility for his or her own behavior that change becomes possible.

There are of course many obvious ways in which one can directly contribute to one's own physical well-being, or lack thereof, by decisions around diet, exercise, tobacco, alcohol and drugs, stress, and fatigue. There are obvious connections between long-term degenerative diseases and lifestyle. But beyond all of this, taking responsibility for the quality of physical health has much more to do with creating possibilities for hope for the future than with assigning blame for the past. This taking of responsibility is a choice that is made at the level of mind and spirit.

Proposition Two: The Family of Origin Has a Singular Influence on Personal Well-Being

The second proposition is that the overall impact of the family-of-origin experience is by far the single most important influence on an individual's personal well-being, including physical health. This is where the inner world of the individual's consciousness (and unconsciousness) of self and the outer world, which is the source of more or less social support for the individual's life, are in a constant circular interaction.

First, there is accumulating evidence that the degree to which hope for the future is present (Sagan, 1987), and the degree to which *personal authority*, defined as "differentiation with intimacy" (Williamson, 1991), is present in the inner consciousness of the individual, one can predict the level of his or her vulnerability to physical illness (Bray, Harvey, & Williamson, 1987). Second, and as noted, the ongoing character of the outer world (i.e., a person's social experience in life, especially the degree to which social support is available) is in constant interaction with the individual's inner construction of reality.

The degree of social support present is a significant and measurable variable that has great influence on vulnerability to physical illness. First, *social support* consists of the presence of a continuing relationship in which the individual feels loved, acknowledged, and listened to. (It is worth noting that the most powerful predictor of clinical depression in a married adult is the statement "I cannot talk to my spouse"; Coyne, 1991.)

Beyond the primary love relationship and other confidants, social support refers in a more general sense to the availability of help. Examples would be the availability of others to provide crisis transportation, child care, and shopping when an individual is in special need. The multiple potential effects of stress on physical health have also been well documented (Justice, 1988). But it has been demonstrated that adequate social support can buffer the effects of ongoing stressors in an individual's life, so that the stress will be less lethal in its physical impact (Williamson & Noel, 1990). The effects that an unusual amount of life change has on physical health have also been shown compellingly (Holmes & Rahe, 1967). The availability or unavailability of social support from the family of origin will have a telling effect at such times.

Again, the constant reciprocal and circular interaction between the individual's inner and outer worlds is manifested. Personal well-being is a social and interactional, not simply an individual, phenomenon. The degree of good hope present in an individual's inner life, and the degree of reciprocating social support present in that person's outer world, are both likely to be significantly influenced by the character of the family-of-origin experience.

Influence of the Family of Origin on Individual Health

With few exceptions, the family-of-origin experience probably has more influence on a person's physical health than any other one source. There are three distinct reasons why this is likely to be so.

First, there is genetic heritage (i.e., the transmission of biological weaknesses, predispositions, and vulnerabilities, as well as strengths). The simple perusal of a patient's medical genogram (J. Rogers, 1990) shows how disease patterns and susceptibilities cross the generations, presumably carried in the genes. If nothing much can be done about this in advance of birth, certainly much of value can be learned later by the adult to help shape his or her future health. Health information need not be received with passive and helpless resignation. Rather, these are cues to help focus one's self-healing attention and energy where they may be most needed.

Second, one must consider the impact of parental modeling of health-care practices, and whether this is a positive or negative influence. Each parent models either a more or a less healthy lifestyle, and also incarnates a particular pattern of attitudes toward and beliefs about health and illness. This ranges from parents for whom illness in the self (or in a member of this family) is simply unthinkable and so rarely occurs, to those who are highly hypochondriacal or given to frequent somatizing. The latter may feel it necessary to recruit repeated surgical procedures paradoxically as a way to ease the pain in their lives. These patterns are likely to have a profound influence on the ways in which the members of the next generation approach physical health.

Third, a considerable amount of unconscious social learning and attitude formation about physical health occurs within the family of origin during children's developmental years. When a child is "chosen" to be the identified patient, he or she can exercise this role through repeated physical illnesses and physical symptoms. In subtle ways, children may be taught how to be sick and how to think of the self as sick, and sick with what outcomes. From a fearful or overprotective parent, a child may learn to feel constantly vulnerable to illness, so that this threat and the resulting fear are always at hand. A child may not only be encouraged, but in subtle ways be rewarded for being sick. Frequently, this is a way to maintain family homeostasis or to maintain stability within either the parental marriage or the internal psychological organization of a parent.

In some families, illness, although a great burden, may also be "welcomed" as a great challenge that gives new meaning and purpose to life. In a few families, illness is embraced with stoic relief. The other shoe has finally dropped. In this way, a child will occasionally discover that he or she has been "chosen" for a career of illness or threats of illness. This sense of self as a special sacrifice may be internalized during the developmental years. These learned, but less than joyful, health behaviors and attitudes are then likely to be re-created within the primary relationship in the next generation, and taught to children in the third generation. By sharp contrast, in some families, physical illness is simply not part of the mythology that formalizes and transmits the mores and morals of this family. In many of these instances, parents model and teach good health practices and lifestyles, and perhaps hardiness and resilience, both intentionally and unwittingly. In their own adult years, these children will recall images of parental well-being and resourcefulness, and can draw strength from these memories, both routinely and in times of stress or crisis.

Proposition Three: Relationships with Health Professionals Re-Create the Emotionality of Family-of-Origin Experiences

The third proposition is that key health professionals—such as primary-care physicians, psychotherapists, and clergy, and especially those who are present in an individual's life over a significant period of time—take on for the patient or parishioner some of the psychological characteristics of parents. They may be experienced as nurturing, or disappointing and withholding. In either case, there is a frequent re-creation of psychological elements of the family-of-origin experience in these interactions. This is likely to lead to intense emotional reactivity. All this underscores the crucial importance of the psychological nature of the doctor–patient relationship.

This is so critical to physical health that it must be discussed further. When it comes to physical health, the key relationship will be with the physician, usually a primary-care physician, with whom a patient has the most consistent and repeated contact over time. Trust and wisdom will be invested in this physician, and a "transference" relationship will be developed. Like all transference relationships, this will include both positive and negative feelings, and ideally the positive will be dominant most of the time. This relationship, like all relationships, is constructed, preferably intentionally crafted, and then sustained through the use of language.

Language is critical because it is used to create the relationship, as well as to debrief the patient about symptoms and other relevant experiences and give feedback, explanation, guidance, and support. Persisting positively and negatively emotionalized memories about parents will clearly influence the ways in which the physician is perceived and related to, and the ways in which his or her language is heard, interpreted, and assimilated. When the physician also "finds" a parent showing up in the psychology of the patient, obviously the plot thickens further and the stage is set for some interesting drama. This helps explain why there is so much declaration of patient dissatisfaction with physicians, second only perhaps to public disappointment with the behavior of clergy persons and the social experience available in churches.

The importance of the ways in which physicians use language to transact business with patients is highlighted by psychotherapy theory's recent focus on the incredible power of suggestion (Erickson & Rossi, 1979). Although chosen with benign intention, it is quite remarkable the degree to which medical language in common usage is laced with negative suggestion. Anxious to avoid clinical mistakes, the practice credo is usually "guilty until proven innocent," that is, until no medical problems or pathology can be confirmed. Even then, patients are cautioned to remember that this good news is only about today, and could change overnight. Complicating matters further, when the patient care offered by the physician is wed to his or her entrepreneurial ambitions—whether this occurs consciously or unconsciously—a language of further engagement and continuing concern may ensue. This interaction is even more likely to be laced with negative suggestion, and therefore not necessarily in the patient's best interest. Professional insecurity, the need to be and to be seen to be in control, and an undue entrepreneurial interest in the process can all encourage, however unwittingly, an increased use of negative suggestion by the physician. Rarely is the speaker aware of the power, and sometimes far-reaching effects, of negative suggestion.

Studies also demonstrate the importance of sensitivity to the "locus of control" issue in the doctor–patient relationship (Holloway & Rogers, 1991). Some patients do better when the health professional takes more control. Other patients do better when their autonomy and responsibility are acknowledged and affirmed. A physician sensitive to and skilled in the nuances of language will be attentive to these distinctions and will have enough internal flexibility to make fine-tuned discriminations in judgment, and therefore in behavior.

All of this demonstrates how critical language skills are in doctor–patient relationships, especially in primary care, because the large majority of patients has not yet developed chronic or life-threatening illness. At the heart of the art of medical conversation is the ability to craft language—first to bond well with patients, and then to select words that transmit information effectively and with empathic overtones. Such a skilled language will also recruit the patient's psychological and spiritual resources on behalf of his or her own well-being. The degree to which a given physician chooses to allow adequate time, and create inner emotional space for this kind of practice, will be determined largely by his or her personal way of showing up in the world, in combination with his or her understanding of the processes of health and illness and good medical care. These two variables are in constant circular reciprocal interaction with one another.

This means that effective physicians will learn alternatives to what is usually thought of as an "objective neutral stance" when engaging in patient care. They will be comfortable behaving as a patient's advocate, openly expecting, promoting, and encouraging the patient's well-being. Actively expecting a patient to be well is a most telling form of positive suggestion. Creating an expectation of good outcomes is the essence of effective psychotherapy, and equally the essence of good medical practice. Expecting a good outcome does not necessarily imply the achievement of the desired outcome. However, it usually expresses a confidence that the patient has the resources to cope well with whatever the future brings. This is a powerful message to the patient, but can only come from a physician with good hope in his or her own heart.

For a physician to be able to craft language effectively, just like the psychotherapist, he or she must learn to listen effectively. This means being able to get the important messages being transmitted by the patient, both the content and the emotion, not just through, but also beneath—and sometimes even despite—what is being said. This is the skill of learning to grasp what C. Rogers (1951) long ago called "the internal frame of reference of the client," the supreme vantage point from which to understand him or her.

In all probability, much harm has been done, usually unwittingly, by physicians who do not know how to bond with and talk effectively to patients. Initially this harm is psychological and spiritual in character, but it may have detrimental physical effects as well. Patients should obviously be protected from physicians who do not have the necessary clinical knowledge and skills. But patients should also be protected, especially in critical watershed moments, from physicians who do not have the necessary relational and language skills to serve them well.

We are also learning more about the power of "therapeutic touch" (Siegel, 1986). Most of the time in patient-care visits, the physician will make some physical contact with the patient. Given personal comfort, sensitivity, and an empathetic presence on the part of the physician, a conscious further touch for a moment or two can constitute a "therapeutic touch," or what religious tradition might call "a laying on of hands." For these reasons, therapeutic psychology in general, and family psychology in particular, have much to contribute to an understanding of the art of patient care in medicine.

The persisting question is: How do we grow physicians (not to mention psychotherapists) with these sensitivities and skills? This kind of practice will place much more demand on the person of the therapist, medical or otherwise. The good news is that repeated conversations with primary-care physicians have convinced the author (Williamson, 1992) that this kind of practice is profoundly more personally satisfying to the practitioner, as well as more effective for the patient. Yet the question continues: How do we get to there from here? This leads to the fourth and final proposition of this chapter.

Proposition Four: A Systemic Orientation to Health and Health-Care Practice Is a Step Toward the Healing of the Mind–Body Split Within the Self

Evidence abounds that the mind–body split has had a disastrous effect on theory and education, and therefore on practice in the health-care disciplines. No further argument or illustration is required here. As noted earlier, this logical question remains: Is there any recourse or alternative at hand? The response of this writer, by no means original, is to suggest that a thorough-going systemic orientation to health and health care holds considerable promise for therapeutic changes in therapeutic practices.

A systemic understanding of the individual patient—which acknowledges the constant correlations and interactions among physical, emotional, and spiritual processes—makes a fine starting point. In a systemic orientation to individual health, the core focus settles on the inner consciousness or psychospiritual stance of a person. This includes the ways in which he or she constructs and reconstructs personal reality, and creates patterns of meanings around day-to-day life experiences. Of particular importance are the myths created around personal health. Out of all this one makes sense of, organizes, and sustains day-by-day living (see Proposition One).

This systemic approach to the individual will be greatly enriched by a systemic understanding of the individual family members' health experiences because these occur within and outwardly express family dynamics and family emotionality. For example, there is considerable evidence of how marital conflict can adversely affect the health of married adults (Doherty & Campbell, 1988). A systemic approach will explore the ways in which the social context of the family supports or adversely affects the physical health of family members. This context either promotes a sense of well-being, which resists illness and enables speedier recovery, or lowers resistance and retards recovery. A systemic orientation will also consider the impact on the individual of the social context of work, with all the inherent possibilities for stress, job insecurity, fatigue, abuse, and an overwhelming sense of failure. By contrast, high job satisfaction encourages personal well-being.

Finally, from a larger ecosystemic perspective, the environment is a biopsychosocial, economic, and cultural context that holds diverse forces and influences that usually simultaneously encourage both wellness and illness. Environmental factors will range from second-hand smoke and toxic infectious agents, through family- and work-related stress, to aspects of the political and cultural milieu, such as sexism, racism, and fascism. Attempts to construct a comprehensive systemic diagnosis and create a systemic treatment plan will quickly seem grandiose, unwieldy, and impractical. The challenge is to have a systemic perspective, and to combine it with an ability to make highly discriminating judgments, and therefore highly focused interventions, and to do it in a short time. The treatment question is always this: Where is the most critical, available, and effective point of therapeutic intervention? This leads to "the big question."

The Big Question

The big question now stares us in the face. This is, how does a professional person move from a linear to a systemic approach to health care and human well-being, whether he or she approaches the question from a medical, psychological, or religious perspective?

Acquiring this systemic perspective is no easy task. We live in a bifurcated world, where reality is split and consciousness is divided. We organize meanings around dynamic opposite poles, such as God and the devil, good and evil, day and night, male and female, black and white, north and south, and, sadly, body and mind. Is a constant war of opposing tendencies the law of nature? Or is it simply that we have chosen to construct reality as to give this appearance? In either event, faced with these polarities, we tend to see the world (and personal life) in what might be loosely called *materialistic* or *spiritual terms*. In the narrowed context of the health-care system, this polarity shows up as the biomedical perspective being pitted against the psychosocial perspective, and vice versa. At one extreme, the biomedical disciple is tempted to see the body as a functionally autonomous machine, subject to mechanical breakdown and repair. The patient's "consciousness" has little place here, except as a potential barrier to compliance, and therefore an irritant and hindrance to the professional. In that case, thank God for anesthesia.

At the other extreme, the psychosocial disciple is tempted to be attentive to a disemboweled, although complex, band of family emotionality ungrounded in biology. Subsequently, professional identity, with inevitable effects on the ability to perform, and personal security can become wrapped up in defending one's chosen point of view. In defending the point of view, one may have the subjective experience of fighting for one's life. How then can transforming change possibly occur?

For example, how does the medical practitioner integrate, or at least relate, contemporary "hi-tech" medicine with a focus on more "natural" healing methods, such as nutrition, homeopathic remedies, bodywork, meditation and prayer, and talking therapy? In general, can professionals in the health-care industry be expected to have the breadth of knowledge, never mind the personal flexibility, to move easily between alternative, and what sometimes appear to be contradictory, truths and realities? Can health-care professionals be expected to have enough personal and professional security and flexibility to be able to tolerate such extreme ambiguity and uncertainty, and still be able to function congruently and effectively in their professional roles?

In the opinion of this writer, the answer to this question is built on where it is that the health professional stands today as an adult, in his or her continuing emotional relationships with the members of his or her family of origin. This refers most especially to the parents, whether alive or deceased. The development of personal authority in life is an alternative to the need to have the illusion of "objective reality." It is an alternative to the need for a dependence—worthy but external (i.e., to the self) reference point for personal truth and confidence (Williamson, 1991). It is not that the practitioner who exercises personal authority has no specific beliefs or convictions about anything. By contrast, this person should be showing a higher level of differentiation in everyday behavior. Rather, he or she has the inner security and flexibility to function effectively in the midst of ambiguity. It is as if he or she knows that his or her beliefs are the "most true" for him or her, which is to say the most professionally useful, among the alternatives available. At the same time, he or she remains open to "new" or evolving "truth."

The professional who can practice his or her art skillfully despite ambiguity, and do so with an "as if" certainty, will be able to move comfortably between different "levels of consciousness" or experience. These will include the biological and the psychological (or psychospiritual). This will be true even where there is polarization and apparent contradiction between objective and subjective, databased and intuitive, and linear and systemic. Every experienced physician who has provided direct patient care—especially in primary-care medicine and preventive medicine—knows from painful experience that this practice is not a science, but an art. But this art is informed by science and guided by verifiable and verified data. Because the systemic interactive processes of health cannot be adequately understood or predicted at any one level, some degree of ambiguity is always present. If nothing else, there is frequently a degree of ambiguity as to the patient's commitment to being well. Therefore, getting or not getting the desired therapeutic outcomes probably pertains more to fluctuations in the art than in the science of medical practice.

Hence, the thesis of this chapter is that the ability to practice this "ambiguous art" effectively and with more congruence than discomfort will be correlated positively with higher levels of personal authority in the physician (Williamson, 1991). However, adequate personal authority is not enough in and of itself. As suggested earlier, freedom from professional dogma and ideology is essential, whatever shape, form, or direction these might take.

Personal Authority and Professional Performance

Step one toward this goal is to locate responsibility within the self, for both personal and professional truth and for the consequences that flow from these, while simultaneously staying in intimate contact with others. In the professional realm, *others* specifically means colleagues as well as patients and their families. Step two, which goes in tandem with this, is freedom from the yearning for a total objectivity, which is to say an externally located truth by consensus. This yearning inevitably leads to ideology and fundamentalism, whether this is masked as religion or science. "Revelation," whether it comes mystically from the mountain tops or logically from controlled experimentation, is subject to interpretation.

The health professional is likely to be less emotionally reactive, which is the precondition of being more objective, when he or she has accepted that there is no way to be present in a clinical situation and yet come from a position that is outside the system. As supervisors and even consultants know, to observe the system is to join it, even if one's conversation about it is only with the self.

Given the fulfillment of these two steps, it is remarkable with what systemic artistry a physician can practice his or her trade. On a few occasions, this writer has had the good fortune to observe this. I describe one memorable example. While listening to a patient's heart sounds and lungs, a physician was intermittently chatting with the patient about how the new marriage was doing, what was proving to be most difficult about it, and how things were going for the patient at work. This symphonic display was followed by a sit-down conversation about the patient's own health expectations—a great clue, incidentally, to the patient's unconscious intentions about her future health. A concluding chat focused on the patient's hopes for good and better things in her life, and an inquiry as to what plans, if any, she thought a "higher power," if she believed in such, might have for her future health. This latter exploration acknowledged the psychospiritual dimension of health, and explored its relevance to this particular patient's well-being. (Obviously, a conversation like this makes certain positive assumptions about the quality of the doctor–patient relationship.) This entire interview took about 19 minutes. The barrier to this kind of practice, assuming the patient is up for it, is not so much lack of time as lack of comfort and skill on the part of the professional.

Yet this kind of systemic exam-room conversation obviously cannot, and indeed should not, characterize every patient visit. The accomplished physician who shares the perspective and values implicit in it will not only be capable of it, but will have a fine-tuned discrimination as to when to use it. This requires a judgment about whether the physician is up for it this day, not simply the patient. Again, it should be obvious how much therapeutic psychology in general, and family systems theory in particular, have to contribute to both primary and graduate medical education.

The health professional (whether medical, psychological, or "allied") who adopts a systemic perspective on his or her practice, unless unusually well located, is likely to be overwhelmed at times by a sense of paddling upstream in the local professional culture. At this point, there is something to be learned from a story about Mother Theresa. There are so few women in her religious community that they make no noticeable dent on the world of the homeless. In relation to this, she was asked why she keeps on doing what she is doing. She replied that she does not at all do what she is doing to heal the world of all those sick and dying on the streets. Rather, she does what she is doing so that she can experience her life in this particular way.

Thus, perhaps the major benefit (for the health professional) of embracing a systemic awareness and systemic approach to practice is that this can be a source of profound personal healing. It can be an important step toward the resolution of the inner divisions that create a fragmented or divided, rather than an integrated, sense of self. Individual consciousness—that moment-by-moment sense of self—is all that one ever has in life. At least this is true within the boundaries of one's own experience. There is great value, then, in a systemic orientation that opens both mind and heart, and that moves toward healing the body–mind split within the personal self, and the psychosocial–biomedical split if that shows up within the professional self. This orientation encourages an appreciation of the interconnectedness and interdependency of all living systems, described by physicist Capra (1989) as "a spiritual awareness."

Conclusion: A Matter of Life and Death

This healing of splits within the self can set the stage for resolving the ultimate bifurcation—the awareness of the starkly different conditions known as *life* and *death*, and the apparent harsh boundary between them. Through what might be called an *experiential systemic embrace of the self*, as a moving part within multiple systems within systems, the bifurcation between life and death may come to seem less radical, more natural, and less frightening.

There is something profoundly healing in being able to distinguish between *observed* and *observer* or *creature* and *creator* within whatever tradition or absence thereof one gives meaning to such words. For this writer, it means that one is free to give up the illusion that there is, somewhere to be found, a Tree of Knowledge, by eating the fruit of which we too shall become as gods, knowing good from evil. Whether the fruit is eaten in the professional, social, political, or religious domain, the effects are not life giving.

The most likely outcome is ideology and fundamentalism, and a loss of self and freedom.

The all powerful family of origin, which for so long may have remained the central dynamic in personal well-being, may now take its place as a favored but less dominant element in the larger human community, into which each one has been born. The suggestion that one is born into a family to leave it takes on new meaning. But it may now be received with more ease, and less disease. The understanding of human health and well-being becomes simultaneously more complex and more simple. So, what else is new?

References

Bray, J. H., Harvey, D. M., & Williamson, D. S. (1987). Intergenerational family relationships: An evaluation of theory and measurement. *Psychotherapy, 24*, 516–528.

Capra, F. (1989, August). *Social construction of reality: How we create values and beliefs.* Unpublished notes from speech given at 27th annual conference of the Association of Humanistic Psychology, Stanford University, Stanford, CA.

Cousins, N. (1989). *Head first.* New York: Dutton.

Coyne, J. (1991, March). *Stress and marital health.* Presentation to Society of Teachers in Family Medicine, Task Force on the Family in Family Medicine, Amelia Island, FL.

Doherty, W. J., & Campbell, T. L. (1988). *Families and health.* Newbury Park, CA: Sage.

Erickson, M. H., & Rossi, E. L. (1979). *Hypnotherapy: An exploratory casebook.* New York: Halsted.

Holloway, R. L., & Rogers, J. C. (1991). Physician adaptation to patients' locus of control and congruence with health recommendations. *Health Communication, 4*(1).

Holmes, T. H., & Rahe, R. H. (1967). The social readjustment rating scale. *Journal of Psychosomatic Research, 11*, 213–218.

Justice, B. (1988). *Who gets sick?* New York: St. Martins Press.

Rogers, C. (1951). *Client centered therapy: Its current practice, implications and theory.* Boston: Houghton Mifflin.

Rogers, J. C. (1990). The self administered program. In R. E. Rakel (Ed.), *Textbook of family practice* (4th ed., pp. 1732–1739). Philadelphia: Saunders.

Siegel, B. (1986). *Love, medicine and miracles.* New York: Harper & Row.

Williamson, D. S. (1991). *The intimacy paradox.* New York: Guilford.

Williamson, D. S. (1992). [Author's conversations with family physicians on the faculty of the Department of Family Medicine, Baylor College of Medicine, Houston, Texas between 1987 and 1992]. Unpublished manuscript.

Williamson, D. S., & Noel, M. L. (1990). Systemic family medicine: An evolving concept. In R. E. Rakel (Ed.), *Textbook of family practice* (4th ed., pp. 61–79). Philadelphia: Saunders.

■ ■ ■